SAINTS
·········· AND ··········
FEASTS
·········· OF THE ··········
CATHOLIC CALENDAR

VOLUME THREE OF FOUR
JULY - SEPTEMBER

SAINTS AND FEASTS OF THE CATHOLIC CALENDAR

VOLUME THREE OF FOUR

JULY - SEPTEMBER

FR. MICHAEL BLACK

Scripture quotations from the New Revised Standard Version Bible: Catholic Edition, copyright © 1989, 1993 National Council of the Churches of Christ in the United States of America. Used by permission. All rights reserved worldwide.

No part of this book not already in the public domain, except for a total of one reflection of one calendar day, may be reproduced or stored, in any form, either in print or digitally, without the prior permission of the publisher. If any copyrighted material has been used in this work without proper credit or attribution being given, please contact the publisher in writing so that future printings may be corrected accordingly.

Cover design by the author and Opus Creative Studio; Interior art by George Angelini, with permission, by Opus Creative Studio, and courtesy of public domain images from the Getty Museum Open Content Program, and Wiki-Commons. Copyright ©2022 Fr. Michael Black, all rights reserved.

TABLE OF CONTENTS

Notes		viii
Poem: It Never Occurred To Me		x
Introduction		1

JULY

Date	Saint/Event	Page
1	St. Junipero Serra	4
3	St. Thomas the Apostle	6
4	Independence Day (U.S.A.)	8
4	St. Elizabeth of Portugal	10
5	St. Anthony Zaccaria	12
6	St. Maria Goretti	14
9	St. Augustine Zhao Rong and Companions	17
11	St. Benedict	19
13	St. Henry	21
14	St. Kateri Tekawitha	23
14	St. Camillus de Lellis	25
15	St. Bonaventure	28
16	Our Lady of Mount Carmel	31
20	St. Apollinaris	33
21	St. Lawrence of Brindisi	35
22	St. Mary Magdalene	37
23	St. Bridget of Sweden	40
24	St. Sharbel (Charbel) Makhluf	42
25	St. James	45
26	SS. Joachim and Anne	47
29	SS. Martha, Mary, and Lazarus	49
30	St. Peter Chrysologus	51
31	St. Ignatius	54

AUGUST		**Page**
1	St. Alphonsus Ligouri	58
2	St. Eusebius of Vercelli	60
2	St. Peter Julian Eymard	62
4	St. John Vianney	65
5	Dedication of the Basilica of Saint Mary Major	67
6	The Transfiguration of the Lord	69
7	St. Sixtus II and Companions	71
7	St. Cajetan	73
8	St. Dominic	75
9	St. Teresa Benedicta of the Cross	78
10	St. Lawrence, Deacon	80
11	St. Clare	82
12	St. Jane Frances de Chantal	85
13	SS. Pontian and Hippolytus	87
14	St. Maximiliam Kolbe	89
15	The Assumption of the Blessed Virgin Mary	91
16	St. Stephen of Hungary	93
19	St. John Eudes	96
20	St. Bernard of Clairvaux	99
21	St. Pius X	101
22	Queenship of the Blessed Virgin Mary	103
23	St. Rose of Lima	105
24	St. Bartholomew	107
25	St Louis	109
25	St. Joseph Calasanz	112
27	St. Monica	114

| 28 | St. Augustine | 116 |
| 29 | The Passion of St. John the Baptist | 118 |

SEPTEMBER		**Page**
3	St. Gregory the Great	122
5	St. Mother Teresa of Calcutta	124
8	The Birth of the Blessed Virgin Mary	127
9	St. Peter Claver	129
12	The Holy Name of the Blessed Virgin Mary	132
13	St. John Chrysostom	133
14	Exaltation of the Holy Cross	135
15	Our Lady of Sorrows	137
16	St. Cornelius	139
16	St. Cyprian	141
17	St. Robert Bellarmine	143
17	St. Hildegard of Bingen	145
19	St. Januarius	147
20	St. Andrew Kim Tae-gŏn & Paul Chŏng Ha-sang, and Companions	149
21	St. Matthew	152
23	St. Pio of Pietrelcina	154
26	SS. Cosmas and Damian	157
27	St. Vincent de Paul	155
28	St. Wenceslaus	159
28	St. Lawrence Ruiz and Companions	161
29	SS. Michael, Gabriel & Raphael, Archangels	163
30	St. Jerome	165

NOTES ON VOLUME THREE AND THIS SERIES

❖ Many saints and blesseds are the official patrons of more than one place, activity, thing, or class of people. Many saints and blesseds are also, by custom or mere digital rumor, the unofficial patrons of various other places, activities, things, or classes of people. The saintly patronages cited herein are accurate but not exhaustive. Some more obscure saints lack any patronage at all.

❖ Spellings of saint and place names are often according to their original language, but not exclusively so.

❖ The cover of Volume III shows, in clockwise order, simulated passport stamps, with their corresponding feast days, for St. Theresa Benedicta of the Cross, St. Kateri Tekawitha, St. Maximilian Kolbe, St. Pio of Pietrelcina, and St. Lawrence of Brindisi. The cover design conveys a sense of the Church's geographical and chronological reach. As the reader briefly immerses herself in the lives of individual saints, she will cross the borders of Europe, Asia, the Americas, and Africa. She will move up and down the centuries, walking the international terrain of the universal Church to briefly meet the friends of God whose deep faith and iron clad virtue shone so brightly both in times long past and, through the liturgy, even today. It is hoped that the cover implicitly conveys that to be an informed Catholic is to be a wise, well-travelled, two- thousand-year-old person. It is to be not just a citizen of the world as it is, but of the world as it was and always will be.

❖ Although the word "feast" is commonly used indiscriminately to refer to any holy day, the Church uses more precise categories: *Solemnity, Feast, Memorial,* and *Optional Memorial.* On certain days of Lent and Advent, a *Memorial* has traditionally been referred to as a *Commemoration.* The Church does not, however, officially use the term *Commemoration* apart from All Souls Day. The liturgical designations cited herein are accurate, though not as fully elaborated as in an Ordo. The subtleties by which the Catholic liturgical calendar operates are not detailed.

❖ The dates of birth and of death of some saints are either totally unknown or disputed by different sources. The letter "c" stands for the Latin *circa*, "about," and is employed when the saint's specific dates are unknown. When a date is disputed among reputable sources, the date given in *Butler's Lives* is generally cited, although not always so.

❖ The "Catholic Calendar" of the title refers, more specifically, to the sanctoral calendar of the Roman Missal, Third Typical Edition, 2002 (English Language Edition 2011). Saint and feast days inserted into the universal sanctoral calendar subsequent to 2011 by the Congregation for Divine Worship and Discipline of the Sacraments are incorporated into this series through the end of 2021. The liturgical calendar of the United States Conference of Catholic Bishops, which adds some North American saints to the universal calendar, is normative for this series.

❖ Thousands of men and women have been canonized by the Congregation for the Causes of Saints and its predecessor Congregations. Many saints, however, date from the pre-Congregation era of the first millennium, when popular acclamation, local episcopal approbation, or long custom were sufficient to confer the title "saint." Only a small percentage of all these stars of holiness shine brightly enough to be included on the Church's universal calendar. It is precisely this constellation of "all-star" saints, and only those saints, who are presented in this series, rather than every single saint known to the Church's long history.

IT NEVER OCCURRED TO ME…

It never occurred to me….

That God would be more than three but less than one.

That Christ's resurrection would not prove death's battle won.

That sin and virtue were not the only things that in the balance hung.

It never occurred to me…

To marvel at the Creator's handiwork but his person shun.

To say I know enough of God and not His depths to plumb.

To choose a broken clump of earth over the landmass to which it clung.

It never occurred to me…

To be grateful to God in silent heart yet leave His song unsung.

That a man think paradise the finish line for a race he did not run.

To not love a church where past sinful tolling can by Christ's hand be unrung.

It never occurred to me…

That Mary would have another son.

To be redeemed by anything but blood.

That Christ's sacred white body could not, would not, rest on my moist red tongue.

M.B.

INTRODUCTION

We learn more from concrete examples than from silken words. The in-your-face impact radiating out from a living, breathing man or woman is without equal. Personal example is a steel fist denting your psyche. When we want to become good and great and holy, when we set out to acquire virtues, we shouldn't marinate in the blue glow of a screen or gaze at puffy castles in the clouds. That's not real life. If we want to get holy, we first have to get real, and there is nothing more real than the lives of the saints.

Holiness is not a warm fuzzy feeling or a good intention. The Church is not an electric blanket warmly comforting us whenever we plug her in. In volume three of *Saints and Feast Days of the Catholic Calendar* we continue reading about the heroic deeds of the Church's all-star team, the best of the best. Some of these men and women were high-profile, others low-profile and still others no-profile. Yet all possessed virtues in abundance. And a virtue is more than one good deed. It is a habit formed from a pattern of good deeds, each one a fortified link in a moral chain.

People are saints not because of their actions, but because of their habits. And those habits are developed through practice. We become good by doing good, just as we become patient not by thinking about patience but by actually exercising patience in real life. Saintliness cannot be divorced from virtuous behavior. Many saints showed astounding bravery in accepting extreme suffering and death, in going on daring missionary journeys, or by forsaking family wealth and prestige to live radical poverty. But great men and women are sometimes defined by small things too – the sharp word unspoken, the subtle gesture few notice, the anonymous generosity revealed only after death.

What do these saints of "smallness" teach us? They teach us that consistency, long suffering, and ordinary fidelity are the stuff of saints too. They teach us that great or dire circumstances are not the only forums for proving holiness. One forum for holiness could be the crowd in the arena lusting for blood. But another forum could be the dinner table where the last juicy steak is passed over and offered to someone else. One forum could be protesting in front of an abortion clinic, while another could be silent adoration of the

Blessed Sacrament in the middle of the night… and not telling anyone about that practice for twenty years.

As much as the Gospels and the Acts of the Apostles inspire the reader with great Christian witnesses, the men and women of the ancient scriptures are not as fully embroidered as man's imagination desires. This explains the popularity of apocryphal literature, private revelation, and modern movies' attempts to add color, contour, and background to the otherwise flat, black-and-white landscape of many well-known New Testament figures. No such apocryphal or imaginative literature has grown up around our post-biblical era saints because no such speculation is needed. We have the facts, the documents, the witnesses, and the stories. We have the triumphs and the tragedies. We know the agonies and the ecstasies.

The lives of the saints place before the reader men and women whose lives can excite in us the holy desire to be like them in specific, attainable ways. The Church canonizes certain holy men and women and enshrines them in a fixed universal calendar simply because this is what the Church is for. The Church does not just teach the truth but is a truth-teaching thing. Our truth-teaching mother exists for many reasons, and one of them is to make her faithful holy in their own unique way, provided that each person's path is blazed according to the Mother's teachings, customs, and time-honored practices. There is, after all, only one Spirit but many individual gifts (1 Corinthians 12:4-11).

JULY

Every man and woman is created ex nihilo to be a saint

JULY

July 1: Saint Junipero Serra, Priest
1713–1784
Memorial; Liturgical Color: White
Patron Saint of California and vocations

"Always forward!" was his motto and his life

The United States of America's impressive Capitol Building in Washington, D.C., includes the majestic, semicircular Statuary Hall. Each of the fifty states chooses two citizens of historic importance to represent it in the Hall. Statues of one nun and four Catholic priests, two of them saints, grace Statuary Hall, including today's saint. Junipero Serra was the founder of California. He was the pathbreaking, indestructible priest who trekked California's mountains, valleys, deserts, and shores to found nine of its eventual twenty-one missions. California's rugged cattle culture, its luxurious orchards and rolling vineyards, its distinctive Mission architecture, and its blending of Mexican and Native American heritage are the legacy of Father Serra and his Franciscan confreres. The Franciscan city names tell the story: San Francisco, Ventura (Saint Bonaventure), San Luis Obispo, Santa Clara, Our Lady Queen of the Angels (Los Angeles) and on and on. The Franciscans simply made California what it is.

Father Junipero Serra was baptized as Michael Joseph on Mallorca, an island in the Mediterranean off the coast of Spain. He grew up dirt poor and devoutly Catholic. He joined the Franciscans as a youth and moved to the large city of Palma de Mallorca, where he took the religious name of Junipero in honor of one of Saint Francis of Assisi's first followers. After priestly ordination, Father Junipero obtained a doctorate in philosophy and taught Franciscan seminarians. He was destined to lead a successful life as an intelligent, holy, and pious intellectual. But in the Spring of 1749, he felt the Lord calling him to become a missionary to New Spain (Mexico). On the fateful day of his departure from his large Franciscan monastery, he kissed the feet of all his brother Franciscans, from the oldest to the youngest. He then boarded a ship and sailed away from his native island for the first time and the last time. He would never see his family again. Our saint's life began in earnest in middle age. Long years of intellectual, spiritual, and

JULY

ascetic preparation steeled his body, mind, and will for the rigors to come.

Arriving in the port of Veracruz, Father Serra walked hundreds of miles to Mexico City rather than travel on horseback. Along this first of many treks, he was bitten by either a snake or a spider and developed an open wound that never healed, causing him near constant pain for the rest of his life. Father Serra spent the first several years of his missionary life in a mountainous region of Central Mexico among an indigenous population that had encountered Spaniards, and the Catholic religion, two centuries before. Father Serra wanted a rawer missionary experience. He wanted to meet and convert pagans who knew nothing of Christianity. After years of faithful service as a missionary, church builder, preacher, and teacher in Central Mexico, Father Junipero finally had his chance. The Franciscans were tasked with leading the religious dimension of the first great Spanish expedition into Alta California, the present day American state. If Father Serra had never gone to California, he may still have been a saint, but one known to God alone. It was the challenge of California that made Father Junipero into Saint Junipero.

Already in his mid-fifties, Father Serra was the head priest of a large migration of men, women, soldiers, cattle, and provisions whose goal was to establish Spanish Catholic settlements in California. Integral to this cultural and evangelical effort was the founding of California's missions, the vast farms, cattle ranches, churches, communities, and schools that have left such an enduring mark on California. For the last fifteen years of his life, Saint Junipero was seemingly everywhere in California—walking, confirming, working, building, preaching, fasting, planning, sailing, writing, arguing, founding, and praying. He exhausted his poor, emaciated body. He was recognized by all as the indispensable man.

Father Junipero died quietly at the San Carlos Mission in Carmel just as the United States was becoming a country on the other side of the continent. He did for the West Coast what George Washington and better known founders did for the East Coast. He founded a society, in all of its complexity. Decades later, Americans migrated to far-off California, newly incorporated into the federal union, looking for gold, and were surprised to discover a distinctive culture as rugged, layered, and rich as the one they had left behind.

California's foundational events were distinctly Catholic just as the Eastern colonies' were distinctly Protestant. When ceremoniously inaugurating an early mission, Father Junipero said a High Mass, sang Gregorian chant, processed with an image of the Virgin Mary, and had the Spanish galleons offshore fire their cannons at the consecration. What powerful solemnity! The roots of large regions of the United States run deep into Southern, not Northern, soil, and were watered by the Catholic faith, not dissenting Protestantism. The United States was baptized Catholic but raised Protestant. Father Junipero represents the best of that "other" founding of the United States of America.

Saint Junipero Serra, inspire us to follow your example of physical perseverance, doctrinal commitment, and spiritual discipline for the good of the Church. You were a model priest, missionary, and Franciscan. May we, too, be great in all that we do.

July 3: Saint Thomas the Apostle
First Century
Feast; Liturgical Color: Red
Patron Saint of doubters and architects

'Perhaps' – the crack in the unbeliever's wall of certainty

All unbelievers have a type of faith. They firmly believe in God's non-existence and in the weakness, not wisdom, of trusting in a reality greater than oneself. Atheism is a belief system, though its object of faith is obviously not God but other sacrosanct, secular "doctrines." Yet the unbeliever's secular faith, just like every believer's, is continually tempted by doubt. The unbeliever, whether fixated on a friend's lifeless body in a coffin, dumbstruck while gazing at the vastness of the sea, or just when lying in the dark of night, wonders if he has everything figured out. Although he shows a brave front, the unbeliever secretly doubts. He is not certain. He is threatened. There is always the great "perhaps." Perhaps, just perhaps…the believer is…right. The atheist is under constant assault from faith, primarily from inside himself. Only when trying to quit religion does he realize, painfully, that the drama of being a

JULY

The Doubting Thomas
Jacopo Palma

man cannot be avoided. He exchanges the uncertainty of belief for the uncertainty of unbelief.

Today's saint, known as "Doubting Thomas," is Christianity's icon of doubt. He loves, serves, and follows the Lord. Upon hearing of the death of Lazarus, Christ decides to go to Judea, where He had previously come under attack. The Apostles are concerned for Christ's safety, but Thomas supports Him, saying, "Let us also go, that we may die with him" (Jn 11:16). Thomas is strong and generous. But he is also a man, so he does what men do—he doubts. Christ's crucifixion was a searing experience for His Apostles, and Thomas doubts that one so cruelly and publicly murdered could be alive. He is told by his co-Apostles that the Lord is risen and has appeared to them. Yet still Thomas doubts. He will only believe if he can place his hands in Christ's very wounds.

To satisfy his skepticism, Thomas joins the others and waits patiently on the Sunday after Easter. The risen Lord appears again in the same place. "Peace be with you," He says to all. And then to Thomas himself, "Put your finger here and see my hands...Do not doubt but believe." "My Lord and my God!" is all the flabbergasted Thomas can muster in response (Jn 20:24–29). Thomas' simple declaration of faith—"My Lord and my God!"—is whispered by millions of faithful at the consecration at Mass, words of faith forged from the anvil of doubt.

Doubt is often the starting point, the context, and the invitation to faith for so many modern doubting Thomases. Yet true doubting leads to true searching. And a true search is not perennially open-ended but risks finding what is sought. Saint Thomas' doubt, his moment of weakness, served a higher purpose when Thomas found what he was looking for. The Son of God said "...the kingdom of heaven is like a merchant in search of fine pearls…" (Mt 13:45) and "The kingdom of God is as if someone would scatter seed on the ground…and the seed would sprout and grow, he does not know how" (Mk 4:26–27). The kingdom is not the fine pearl. The kingdom is the merchant *in search of* fine pearls. The kingdom is not the seed. It is the man *scattering* the seed. The search, the scattering, the effort, the struggle, the journey. These are often the first stages of finding God. Honest, authentic inquiry is god-like. Every legitimate search presupposes, after all, that there is something, or someone, to find.

Doubt is the plow that opens the furrow where the seed of faith can fall and germinate. Saint Thomas the Apostle is our guide and patron in understanding how doubt sparks faith. Being absent, he heard. Hearing, he doubted. Doubting, he came. Coming, he touched. Touching, he believed. And believing, he served.

Saint Thomas, help all who struggle with belief in God. Through your example and intercession, assist all those overwhelmed by distractions and doubts to come to a well-informed trust in the Father and Lord of all.

July 4: Independence Day—USA

Optional Memorial; Liturgical Color: White

"...nobis donet en patria."

Father hunger—the primordial longing to impress, to emulate, or just to find dad—moves us more fundamentally than any thirst for mom. Mom's warm love and constant presence is typically assumed. She is always near. We spend the first nine months of life sheltered inside her sanctuary, a memory of closeness and protection buried deep in our psyche. But dad comes later, a remote creature orbiting around mother and child with a deep voice, sandpaper face, and rugged hands. Knowing him, and loving him, takes some work, and for that reason seems more worth it. The desire for a *pater*, a father, goes hand in hand with our need for a *patria*, or fatherland. To be a citizen of the world is not to be a citizen at all. The world is not a country. We don't want to be born at sea, drifting under a flag, any

JULY

more than we want to be born into family. We want to be born into *a* family. We want to master one language, stir upon hearing one hymn, and stand with our civic siblings to honor one flag. We want, and need, to love a *patria*. Independence Day of the United States of America commemorates the founding events of a country as worthy of admiration and appreciation as any country ever was. The United States merits respect for a thousand compelling reasons, but honoring her also points to the inherent limits of even the healthiest love of fatherland.

There are only a few things a man will die for: family, religion, and country being the most obvious. To emigrate to the United States many immigrants have, for centuries now, disrupted family life, bid farewell to well-loved homelands, abandoned historic family farms, and been absent from spouses and children for months and years. Why? Because it was worth it! A country worth dying for is a country worth dying to get into. No country has ever afforded its citizens what America has afforded them. Its success is unequalled. And yet, for all of its flourishing opportunity, robust legal structures, and protection of human rights, the *patria* of the U.S. is not, and no *patria* could ever be, Heaven itself. A country provides meaning, but not ultimate meaning.

When Americans die they will not be judged by Uncle Sam. An old man with a long white beard wearing a star-spangled waistcoat will not stand before the individual soul. Uncle Sam won't judge anyone because Uncle Sam doesn't exist. He is as real as the Easter Bunny, the Tooth Fairy, or Lady Liberty. The Statue of Liberty consists of a rigid iron frame draped in thin copper. That's it. "She" rusts. Meaningful secular holidays invite reflection upon what kind of truth perdures and upon the difference between two close cousins, faith and patriotism. Jesus Christ is not like Uncle Sam. He is not an anthropomorphism, a depiction in human form of a non-human reality. We have statues and paintings of Jesus Christ for the same reason we have statues and paintings of George Washington—because the camera hadn't been invented yet. If there had been cameras in first-century Palestine, Jesus' face would be as correctly shown as Abraham Lincoln's.

Our crucifixes don't symbolize God. They show God. Jesus is not a metaphor. He is not the human representation of ethereal God-like qualities. Jesus thundered with the authority of God, referred to Himself as God, and performed Godly acts, including the ultimate miracle of raising Himself from the dead. Jesus doesn't represent something else, or someone else, that hides behind a curtain or a mask. Our love of God, then, should run deeper than our love of country because God will, by definition, never end. Mighty Rome ended. Weeds grew, and still grow, in the bustling forum where Julius Caesar was knifed in the back. America's raw military power, global cultural reach, and thumping economy will not last forever. Countries rise and countries fall, but God and His Church will endure.

Geological time uses immense spans of millennia, ages, and eons to capture the reality of glacial movement, tectonic shifts, and continental splitting. We should use similar references of time when describing the vastness of God. A two-thousand-year-old Church is ancient of days in man-time. But in God-time the Church is just a babe rocking in a cradle. Geologically we would understand this. Theologically we should as well. The United States will pass into history in one blink of God's eyelashes. So we should love more what deserves more love. We should love less what deserves less love. And we should live more fully only for a deathless God who grants endless life in a true homeland that will never cease.

God the Father, may our hearts bear a deep love for our earthly fatherland as an extension of our love for You, our Father in Heaven. May our one heart burst with love for all those that deserve our love, most especially our family, our nation, and our Church.

July 4: Saint Elizabeth of Portugal
1271–1336
(Celebrated July 5 in the U.S.A.)
Optional Memorial; Liturgical Color: White
Patron Saint of widows and victims of adultery

A widowed queen embraces Sister Poverty

Beautifully placed in the center of a graceful arch, behind the high altar in the Franciscan convent of Saint Clare in Coimbra, Portugal, is an impressive silver and glass sarcophagus. Circular windows cut into the upper portion of the finely wrought box allow the pilgrim to peer down into its contents. You see rumpled printed cloth. You struggle to discern what else you are looking at. But then...you see...the form of a body, covered by a shroud. It is her. You are looking at a sleeping queen, Saint Elizabeth of Portugal. Only a hand protrudes from under the cloth. It is a right hand. It is visible. It is white. It has refused decay. It is incorrupt. The rest of her body? Only God knows, and maybe the local bishop.

Today's saint was also known as Elizabeth of Aragon. She was born into a royal Spanish family with a saint in its bloodline. Saint Elizabeth of Hungary was her great aunt and namesake. In a pious age, the piety of today's Saint Elizabeth stood out. She loved the Lord and all that it meant to be Catholic. She was wed to the King of Portugal at a tender age, moved to his land, and had a family with him. The holy child Elizabeth became the holy adult Elizabeth. She involved herself in matters of war, state, and politics. But she was more concerned with her own soul, the poor, and the sick.

Elizabeth had the luxury of leisure due to her wealth and noble status. She could dedicate time to Mass, to prayer, and to her spiritual exercises. Her resources of time and money also allowed her to assist the poor, which she did generously, even to the annoyance of her husband, the King. It is easy to say that money doesn't matter when you have money. Only people with money, in fact, say that money is not the only thing. Money did not matter to Elizabeth, precisely because she did not lack it. She simply gave it away. And she fortified her financial generosity with her personal example of prayer, fasting, poverty, and holiness, edifying her people. She was not an advocate of social justice, but justice. She did not promote charitable giving, but living charity itself.

After her husband died and her children were grown, she entered the convent of the Poor Clares, which she herself had founded in Coimbra. She took vows as a Third Order Franciscan, abandoned her royal status, and lived in obscurity with the other sisters. Coimbra had a long attachment to the Franciscans. It is the city where Fernando of Lisbon, an Augustinian, decided to become Anthony, a Franciscan, the future saint whose shrine is in Padua. Saint Elizabeth's choice to become a lay Franciscan shows just how far and wide the influence of Saint Francis of Assisi was felt, even among the upper classes. The Queen of Portugal gives away her wealth, cares for the poor and the sick, is devoted to the Sacraments, actively promotes peace in her domain and in her family, establishes a female Franciscan convent, and herself becomes a Franciscan, and all within one hundred years of Saint Francis' death. After Elizabeth had given away all that she had, she gave away herself, and then there was nothing left to give. She was a model Catholic Queen.

Saint Elizabeth of Portugal, help us to see all wealth, of time or money, as a gift and an opportunity to serve the Lord and our fellow man. You promoted peace in your realm and in your family, in the spirit of Saint Francis. Help us to do the same.

<u>July 5: Saint Anthony Zaccaria, Priest</u>
1502–1539
Optional Memorial; Liturgical Color: White
<u>Patron Saint of physicians</u>

The man of the hour for his time and place

In thirty-nine niches in the nave and transepts of St. Peter's Basilica in Rome are thirty-nine statues of saints who founded religious congregations. Some of these saints are very well known, like Saints Benedict, Ignatius of Loyola, and Teresa of Ávila. Today's saint is among the lesser-known founders. The statue of Saint Anthony Zaccaria looks down from a second-tier niche, high above the Basilica floor. Saint Anthony's distance from the faithful in art reflects his relative remoteness from modern life. Not every saint can be a rockstar. The Church preserves the legacy of this holy man on its universal calendar, though, for very solid reasons.

Saint Anthony was born in Northern Italy just as the powder keg of the Protestant Reformation was about to ignite. He studied medicine and became a practicing physician. But his real love was people's souls, not their bodies, and he dedicated most of his time to teaching the catechism to the poor. Like so many priestly vocations, others recognized his gifts before he saw them himself. Friends and family encouraged him to study for the Priesthood. Saint Anthony was ordained in 1528 and soon moved to the bustling city of Milan. He became a roving chaplain to nobles and to diverse lay groups committed to charitable works and to invigorating Milanese society with an authentic Catholic spirituality.

JULY

Along with two noblemen, Saint Anthony founded a Congregation of priests whose goal was to "regenerate and revive the love of divine worship and a properly Christian way of life by frequent preaching and faithful ministering of the sacraments." There is nothing new, creative, or groundbreaking in such goals. But as would be highlighted a few decades after Saint Anthony by Saint Charles Borromeo, the vigorous Archbishop of Milan, Northern Italy in the sixteenth century was in a state of religious decrepitude. Today's saint and his co-founders needed to found a Congregation to blow life into the dormant coals of people's faith and to rekindle their love of the Mass and the Holy Eucharist. No one else was carrying out these fundamental evangelical tasks. The secular clergy were moribund, and bishops often did not even reside in their dioceses. Someone had to do something, and thus the "Clerks Regular of Saint Paul Beheaded" was born and formally recognized in 1535.

The Congregation's members became more commonly known as the Barnabites after a Church in Milan where they were eventually headquartered or perhaps due to Saint Barnabas' status as one of Saint Paul's closest companions. The Barnabites encountered fierce opposition from local clergy who were offended by the imputation that they were derelict in their duties and needed reform. These internecine knife fights were quickly settled in the Barnabites' favor.

Saint Anthony popularized the Forty Hours Devotion, where the Blessed Sacrament is exposed over a three-day period corresponding to Christ's forty hours in the tomb. He encouraged churches to toll their bells on Friday afternoons, and preached indefatigably in the streets on the crucifixion, on the Eucharist, and on the texts of Saint Paul. The age for scholastic theological distinctions as fine as lace had long ended by the early sixteenth century. The one-church world was crumbling and with it the luxury of inter-Catholic speculations of a purely theoretical nature. Dissenting Protestantism was spilling into Northern Italy. What was needed was preaching in the streets, raw fervor, and the core biblical message. Some priests spoke with quiet erudition and convinced the few, others explained the catechism well, but only inside of churches to the scattered faithful in the pews. Saint Anthony's method was, essentially, to walk into the town square, light his hair on fire, and yell "Watch me burn!" It worked—but not for long. Saint Anthony Zaccaria flamed out at the early age of thirty-seven. He was canonized in 1897, and his remains are venerated today in the crypt of the Barnabite church in Milan. The Congregation he founded is of modest size yet still vigorously serving in the heart of the Church.

Saint Anthony Zaccaria, inspire us to do the simple things of our faith well, before we attempt to do the complex things less well. Keep us focused on the events of the Gospel as the Church presents them to us through her structure, her Sacraments, and her devotions.

July 6: Saint Maria Goretti, Virgin and Martyr
1890–1902
Optional Memorial; Liturgical Color: Red
Patron Saint of rape victims and teenage girls

A country girl suffers death for knowing right from wrong

The family of today's saint was so poor that they farmed other people's fields. They lost their own land and became migrant laborers who ate what they grew and harvested, their rough fingers rarely touching a coin or printed money. It was a hardship for the parents to house, feed, clothe, and educate their seven children. And then things got bad. The father died of malaria. The family was now forced to share a modest home with another family, and the mother had to work the fields alongside her children day in and day out. In the midst of all this cruel hardship, tragedy struck.

Maria typically stayed home to cook, clean, sew, and care for her baby sister. It was while she was alone with the baby at home one day, mending a shirt of Alessandro's, the teenage boy of the family that shared the house, that Maria was attacked. Alessandro had returned—and he wasn't looking for his shirt. It was not the first time he had imposed himself on eleven-year-old Maria. And it was not the first time she had refused. She tried to stop him again. She screamed that it was a mortal sin. She yelled that he would go to hell. Alessandro didn't care. She ran for the door, but it was too late. He stabbed her multiple times in the throat, heart, and lungs.

Little Maria was brought to the hospital where doctors tried in vain to save her life. Before dying, she revealed to her mother, and to the police, for the first time, that Alessandro had tried to rape her twice before. Since he had threatened her with death if she told anyone, she had kept silent. Before succumbing to her wounds, Maria forgave her attacker and said she wanted Alessandro to one day be with her in paradise. Maria's last twenty-four hours were dramatic. She explicitly chose death rather than to allow another's mortal sin. She suffered sexual violence like so many female martyrs of the early Church. And on her deathbed, with her body weakening, she forgave her murderer. This was all extraordinary. This was the stuff of saints.

Maria Goretti was canonized in 1950 by Pope Pius XII in St. Peter's Square in Rome. The huge number of the faithful made it impossible to say the Mass inside St. Peter's Basilica. Maria's mother and siblings were at the canonization, as was Alessandro. After initially refusing to communicate with anyone about the murder, he opened up to a local bishop who took the time to visit him in jail. Alessandro told the bishop he had a dream in which Maria presented him with lilies, symbols of purity. But the lovely flowers scorched his hands as soon as he touched them. He later asked Maria's mother, Assunta, forgiveness for his crime. Like her daughter, she forgave him. Alessandro served twenty-seven years of his thirty-year sentence. After being released, he became a lay Franciscan and served as a gardener in a monastery until his death.

Saint Maria showed uncommon maturity for her age. Her poor, rugged life in the fields, and her father's early death, made life itself serious very early on. Starving people are not frivolous. Death, suffering, poverty, migration, and loss figured prominently in her life before she ever even attended school. She knew no comfort apart from the closeness of family life and the security of faith. When she chose to give up her life rather than participate in another's sin, she was not saying goodbye to a beautiful house, creature comforts, or earthly possessions. She had the clothes on her back and sanctifying grace in her soul. Nothing else. That grace was the secret possession she would not trade for life itself. She kept a tight grip on her soul, and God rewarded her tenacity by granting her life in heaven with Him forever.

ST. MARIA GORETTI
July 6

"Yes, I too, for the love of Jesus forgive him."
– *Maria on her deathbed forgiving her murderer.*

JULY

Saint Maria Goretti, mature beyond your years, inspire all young people to value purity and chastity as God-given gifts. Help them to follow your example in valuing virtue over vice, love of God over love of man, and a rich future in heaven over a poor future on earth.

July 9: Saint Augustine Zhao Rong and Companions, Martyrs
1746–1815
Optional Memorial; Liturgical Color: Red

New saints for an ancient land start the Third Millennium

Today's feast commemorates one hundred and twenty martyrs, eighty-seven native Chinese and thirty-three Western missionaries, killed in a long trail of blood from 1648 to 1930. This roll call of heroes includes lay women, catechists, seminarians, bishops, priests, a cook, a farmer, a widow, a seventy-nine-year-old man and a child of nine. Some were killed while taking sanctuary inside of a church. A large number died during the Boxer Rebellion in 1900, when fanatical Chinese peasants slaughtered thousands of Christian converts and foreign missionaries for no reason other than their faith and their foreignness. Some lives were ended by beheading, quickly; others by neglect in prison, slowly; and many by strangulation, painfully.

The one saint the Church names on this feast is Saint Augustine Zhao Rong. Like so many other saints, he began his professional life as a soldier. As part of his military duties, Augustine was assigned to escort a French priest in China. The priest's holy example made such a deep impression on Augustine that he decided to convert to Catholicism. After his baptism, he went for the gold—he entered the seminary and became Father Augustine. His priestly ministry was short lived. Father Augustine was jailed, tortured, and left to die in prison during the reign of an emperor insanely hostile to Christianity and to Chinese priests in particular. Numerous other Chinese and foreigners were swallowed up in the same persecution along with Father Augustine. All refused to apostatize and many were atrociously tortured.

After some faint contact with Christianity in the first millennium, European missionaries first ventured deep into China in the last decades of the 1500s. These missionaries were chosen for their great erudition, sagacity, and Christian spirit. In contrast, the first boatloads of Spanish missionaries unloaded into Latin America were a mixture of holy, educated men, along with others who were almost ordained pirates, adventurers whose zeal for the house of the Lord was so total that they were oblivious to the sensitive cultural realities they, and the West itself, were encountering for the first time. Mayan and Aztec Codexes' were burned, finely carved statues were shoved off temple platforms, and palaces were razed to the ground out of an authentic, but misguided, Christian fervor. No such haphazard cultural destruction took place in China. Missionaries to China were finely tuned to the local wavelength. They learned the challenging language, respected local spiritualities, and were exquisitely respectful of the ancient, studious, and complex society that had welcomed them. These sterling missionaries inspired a large number of Chinese converts who remained fully Chinese while, at the same time, becoming fully Catholic. Catholicism enriched and purified all that it meant to be Chinese.

Yet the missionaries' success was also the seed of their destruction. Chinese strongmen invariably saw the missionaries as agents of Western colonialism rather than as emissaries of Jesus Christ. No matter how delicately the missionaries inculturated the faith, or how many locals converted, Catholicism was a non-native reality that threatened ancient Chinese patterns of life and thought. And so the persecutions came.

The Protomartyr of China was Francis Fernández de Capillas, a Dominican priest who was tortured and beheaded in 1648 while praying the Sorrowful Mysteries of the Rosary. Numerous Franciscans, Salesians, Dominicans, and Jesuits were killed in the intermittent waves of persecution. These martyrs' crime was their faith and energetic evangelical efforts. They were not involved in politics or trade. They were not spies or government agents. They died for the most noble and purest of reasons—their faith. The ancient nation of China had no saints before October 1, 2000, when Pope Saint John Paul II canonized today's Chinese martyrs. Not one of the canonized was killed under the communists who have ruled China since 1949. Catholics executed by the communists await a future unfurling of their banners in St. Peter's Square. More

Chinese martyrs, some already dead, some still to die, will be canonized in an unknown year by a future pope as the history of redemption reveals its secrets.

Martyrs of China, you were brave in keeping a tight grip on the pearl of great price. Help all Christians to value their faith in easy times so that when times of persecution come, we may stand upright in the storm.

July 11: Saint Benedict, Abbot
c. 480–c. 550
Memorial; Liturgical Color: White
Patron Saint of Europe and monks

His Rule helped create Europe, one monastery at a time

Before the time of today's saint, to be a monk meant to wander into the Syrian desert and never come back, to climb a rocky summit in the Sinai and never descend, to sit cross-legged atop a pillar, to fast to emaciation, or to remain wordless as a hermit in a damp cave in Lebanon. Saint Benedict changed all of this. This revolutionary introduced evolutionary change, a new way for monks to be radically committed to Christ. No more would a monk have to perch like a hawk in its eyrie, alone, gazing over the valley below. When Benedict opened his mouth and called the monk out of his desert, down from his mountain, off of his pillar, and out of his cave, monks answered.

Benedict founded Western monasticism, the communities of monks who pray, eat, work, and socialize together in a common chapel, refectory, field, and workshop. Benedictine monks created Europe out of the vacuum of blackness and disorder which enveloped the land after Roman order disintegrated. So many centuries later, the pioneering path that Benedict cut for Western civilization is difficult to appreciate. What was fresh is now ancient. What was revolutionary is now just the way things are.

Little is known with certainty of Saint Benedict's life. No contemporary preserved his essential details, as the great Saint Athanasius did for Saint Anthony of the Desert. Decades after Benedict's death, Pope Saint Gregory the Great recorded some precious few anecdotes of the great monk's life, but the lack of hard facts and historical chronology leave room for speculation. What is known for certain is that he held in his hands what the world had to offer for a few short years and then dropped it like a murder weapon. He would live for Christ and Christ alone. He joined a primitive community of consecrated men for several years but departed after some unspecified intrigues to form his own small monasteries. Exercising spiritual and practical fatherhood over his brother monks, he was inspired to write a Rule. Benedict became famous, in time, not due to a wealth of biographical detail but because of his Rule. Saint Benedict is his Rule and his Rule is him.

The Benedictine Rule came to dominate all of Europe. In a Christian age when monasteries dotted every low valley and high town, when the local abbot was as powerful as the bishop, and when schools and culture were synonymous with monastic learning, these communities almost always lived by the Rule of Saint Benedict. Benedict's Rule became widespread because it was both deeply spiritual and imminently practical. It demanded uncompromising dedication to work and prayer but held individual and community goods in a careful balance.

A Benedictine monastery was not just a place for penance or asceticism but a family. It was a finely tuned orchestra with the abbot waving his wand at the front, eliciting from the monks' individual gifts a common harmony to soothe God and correctly order nature itself. The monastery's structured routine of chanting the Divine Office, of work, of study, of constructing a community for community's sake, gave Europe a finely tuned rhythm that drove technology, the arts, and scholarship forward by leaps and bounds over other lands.

Until the time of Saints Francis and Dominic in the early 1200s, there was only one founder worth noting in the church, and that was Saint Benedict. The immense legacy of the founders of large, powerful, and lasting Orders in the Church is mysterious. Founders influence the Church's spirituality and theology almost as much as Divine Revelation itself. And Benedict was the founder of all founders. Saint Augustine of Hippo, Benedict's only serious competition for the greatest saint of the first millennium, also left a widely adopted rule, but it never produced the unified and practical communities which Benedict's Rule generated. Saint Benedict rests in peace near his twin sister, Saint Scholastica, in a crypt under the historic Monastery of Monte Cassino. The "upper room" of Monte Casino became European culture's symbolic Acropolis and Temple Mount, the beacon to the town, the lighthouse of Western civilization, and it was Saint Benedict who first lit its lamp.

Saint Benedict, you were a humble monk whose life remains largely unknown, yet you left a massive legacy. Help each Christian in his home, church, and workplace to labor from the shadows to create light, to be the unseen cause behind great effects, and to light lamps that guide others through the darkness.

July 13: Saint Henry
973–1024
Optional Memorial; Liturgical Color: White
<u>Patron Saint of the childless and Benedictine Oblates</u>

A king walks the tight path of virtue

Passing through the heroic-sized doors of St. Peter's Basilica in Rome, the pilgrim walks into a vast interior space, his gaze slowly rising to silently absorb the sublime vaults, criss-crossed by ethereal beams of sunlight. Yet as the pilgrim meanders, head tilted upward, eyes drinking in the beauty, he is actually walking on art too. Near the end of St. Peter's central nave, embedded in the elaborate marble floor, is a large, deep red disk. It is porphyry, a rich purple granite prized by the emperors and nobles of Rome. This disk, harvested from an Egyptian quarry, was originally placed in a Roman home or public building. But the Emperor Constantine pilfered it. He had the disk transplanted to near the main altar of the fourth-century basilica he built in honor of Saint Peter, and the disk has been preserved, in a different location, in the present sixteenth-century basilica. And on this lush granite disk numerous kings and emperors, including Charlemagne and today's saint, Henry II, humbly knelt to be crowned by popes. Saint Henry made the long journey from Germany to Rome to be crowned Holy Roman Emperor by Pope Benedict XIII on February 14, 1014. Not just common men but kings too went on pilgrimage to Rome to seek Saint Peter's blessing.

JULY

The Coronation of Saint Henry by Pope Benedict XIII

The life of Saint Henry shows that even a king has a King. Even the powerful are under Someone who is more powerful. Good kings know that; bad ones don't. King Henry lived a life in many ways typical of the royals of his era. He was involved in almost continuous political intrigues and military battles to protect and expand his kingdom. There were fights to attain power and fights to retain power. There were long military campaigns in Poland, Hungary, Germany, and Italy. There was court intrigue, a strategic but childless marriage, the envy of nobles, and all the other ingredients inherent to the struggle for power. But Henry is the only Holy Roman Emperor ever to be canonized a saint for a reason. He had deep faith. He loved the Church. He lived the virtues to a heroic degree. He received the Sacraments. He was devoted to Saint Mary.

Saint Henry was outstanding in utilizing his wealth and position to advance the apostolates of the institutional Church. He formed a new diocese, endowed others, founded monasteries, donated land, and had close relationships with powerful bishops. Under his care, the church became an arm of the imperial government, with bishops of large dioceses even becoming princes wielding both civil and ecclesiastical power. This blurring of the lines between Church and State in Germany became problematic in later centuries when imperial officials tried to wrest church governance from the pope's hands and flexed their secular muscle in crushing heretics. But under Saint Henry the mingling of church and state was mutually beneficial. It created a united love of fatherland and religion, of culture and liturgy, of patriotism and faith, which lasted until the early sixteenth century throughout all of Germany and until the Napoleonic era in large swaths of it.

The rich and powerful are subject to temptations just like the common man, yet their wealth and influence can carve new pathways of sin not open to the common man. So when a king, queen, president, prime minister, multi-millionaire, or movie star walks the straight road and enters through the narrow gate, there is a bit more to celebrate. The sinful road not taken, the evil path that could have been trod but was not, is a cause for rejoicing for every man, but especially for the powerful man. Every soul can indulge in some legitimate Christian pride for what it has not done, for having conquered temptation and sin by strategically avoiding it. Many paths opened up before King Henry during his life. He walked the tight path of virtue and entered heaven by the narrow gate and thus exalted his royal status to one even higher, that of a saint.

Saint Henry, you were an exceptional benefactor of the Church, living sacrificial generosity to advance her apostolates. May your example help us all to be generous, in every way, when our religion demands a generous response.

July 14: Saint Kateri Tekakwitha, Virgin (U.S.A.)
1656–1680
Memorial; Liturgical Color: White
Patron Saint of Canada and orphans

Tough as a hide, pure as a fawn

Kateri (Iroquois for "Catherine") Tekakwitha lived a short life of twenty-four years, the same age attained by Saint Thérèse of Lisieux at her death. Kateri's father was a pagan Mohawk Chief and her mother a Christian Algonquin. The Mohawk people were the easternmost tribe of the larger Iroquois Confederacy. Her younger brother and both of her parents died in a smallpox epidemic which damaged young Kateri's vision and scarred her face. She was taken in by an aunt and an uncle, the Chief of the Turtle Clan, and grew up in their longhouse. Over time she mastered the domestic arts typical of the women of her tribe—fashioning animal skins into belts and clothes, weaving, cooking, and other skills. Kateri was shy, perhaps due to her impaired vision and damaged skin. But she listened carefully. Very carefully. Jesuit missionaries visited her relative's home and taught them about Jesus Christ and the Catholic religion. Kateri was there in the background, sweeping, cooking, and sewing, paying close attention to what the adults were saying around the table, something typical of adolescents in every culture.

More than being converted, Kateri converted herself. After dramatically refusing an arranged marriage, eighteen-year-old Kateri approached a Black Robe, Jesuit Father Jacques de Lamberville, and requested baptism. He guided her through the Catechism. After a few months she told him, "I have deliberated enough. For a long time my decision on what I will do has been made. I have consecrated myself entirely to Jesus, son of Mary, I have chosen Him for husband and He alone will take me for wife." She was baptized in honor of Saint Catherine of Siena on Easter Sunday, 1676.

Soon after her baptism, encountering some resistance from her fellow Mohawks, Kateri left upstate New York and crossed into present day Canada to live close, but not too close, to the French and their religion, in a village called Kahnawake. This was a traditional Iroquois settlement—it survived on fishing, hunting, and farming—with a twist. Its inhabitants were Iroquois Catholics. They did not allow polygamy, premarital sex, divorce, or abuse of alcohol. The Indians did not want to become French but to merge their traditional way of life with their newfound religion. The Jesuits served these Catholic Iroquois from the nearby mission of Sault Saint-Louis. A Jesuit priest's letter from 1682 vividly describes life in Kahnawake and specifically mentions, but leaves unnamed, a young female Mohawk convert of extraordinary piety. It was Kateri.

Kateri and a group of like-minded Mohawk women bonded in a warrior sisterhood that practiced traditional Catholic piety with an indian emphasis on voluntary suffering. These women were as tough as bark. They wanted to emulate the sufferings of Christ, to atone for sins, and to mortify themselves in the tradition of so many great European saints. They wore hair shirts and put on iron belts with small metal spikes. They stood in ice water while praying the rosary. Bearing pain, publicly, was part of their culture and native religion. Catholicism's traditional theology of atonement and mortification melded perfectly with aspects of the Iroquois' native religion.

Kateri was devoted to the Holy Eucharist and Mary. She was reserved and contemplative by nature. She delighted in nature's beauty—in trees, birds, and wildflowers—and gathered these last to decorate the altar for Mass. Kateri remained a virgin and is called the Lily of the Mohawks for her purity. Her delicate health failed her early and she died with the words "Jesus, Mary, I love you" on her lips. Minutes after her death the people at her bedside noticed something. The scars that incised her cheeks were slowly repaired, and her skin became pure, smooth and beautiful. The faithful maiden of the woods had earned her reward.

Saint Kateri, we ask your humble and pious intercession to inspire all young people, especially girls, to attain the virtues which came so easily to you—to be uncomplaining, physically tough, contemplative in spirit, chaste in body, pious, and charitable to all.

July 14 (July 18 U.S.A.): Saint Camillus de Lellis, Priest
1550–1614
In the U.S.A. this Optional Memorial is transferred to July 18
Optional Memorial; Liturgical Color: White
Patron Saint of hospitals, nurses, and the sick

A one-man Red Cross who burned with love for the sick

Like so many saints, Camillus de Lellis ran hard in whatever direction he was heading. When he was a soldier, he ran hard toward the noise of battle. When he was a gambler, he ran hard toward the betting tables. When he was a sinner, he ran hard toward his taste of the day. And when he had a conversion, he ran hard toward the tabernacle. And there, finally, he stopped running. Once he found God, he stayed with Him. Today's saint spent long hours with Christ in the Blessed Sacrament. Silent contemplation fueled his soul, and he motored through each day with a high-octane love for the sick and the dying, which attracted numerous followers, led to the founding of a religious order, and eventually made Camillus a saint.

JULY

As a physically large teenager, Camillus became a soldier, alongside his soldier father, to fight the Turks. In the army he learned to gamble, an addiction that matured with him and which ultimately reduced him to abject poverty. At a low point in his life, he volunteered to work at a Franciscan monastery that was under construction and became inspired by a monk to seek admission to the order. But they wouldn't take him. Camillus had a serious leg wound that refused to heal. He would have been more burden than blessing, so he moved on. He went to Rome to care for the sick in a hospital where he had previously been a patient. But he was repelled by the inadequate medical care, the moral deprivation of the nurses, and the lack of spiritual attention given to the patients. Camillus decided something better was needed for the sick and found the solution when he looked in the mirror.

Camillus was inspired by his saintly spiritual director, Saint Philip Neri, to establish a company of consecrated men who would serve the sick purely out of love for God. They served in the hospital of the Holy Spirit, still found today on the Tiber River close to the Vatican. Camillus and his co-workers earned a reputation for providing excellent medical care, for indefatigable service, and for doing their work with an intense spirit of prayer. While carrying out this demanding apostolate, Camillus also attended seminary and was ordained a priest in 1584. As the years passed, more men joined, new houses were established in other cities, and the rule for the Order of Clerks Regular, Ministers of the Infirm (M.I.), simply known as the Camillians, was approved by the Pope in 1591.

Father Camillus instituted medical reforms that were rare for his time in regard to cleanliness, diet, infectious diseases, the search for cures, and the separation of healthcare administration from healthcare itself. When his order expanded to other countries, they even staffed a medical field unit accompanying soldiers in battle, an important innovation. This, together with his order's habit bearing a large, simple, red cross on the front, made Camillus a precursor of the modern Red Cross.

Saint Camillus was practical as well as mystical. He wanted the best, physically, spiritually, and morally, for all those he cared for. Every patient was his Lord and Master. No patient, no matter how diseased, foul, dirty, or rude, was beyond his care. Along with his

JULY

ST. CAMILLUS DE LELLIS
July 14

"More love in those hands, brother."

– St. Camillus' refrain to his religious brothers as they served the sick in the hospital.

religious brothers, he even took a special fourth vow to care for those with the plague who might infect him. Two Camillians died of the plague in Camillus' own lifetime. "More love in those hands brother" was his constant refrain to his confreres. His example resonated, and the work of the Camillians continues today in various countries.

After his order was firmly established, Saint Camillus succumbed to various diseases in 1614 in Rome. Soon after his death, two doctors from Holy Spirit Hospital came to examine the body, as Camillus was already considered a saint. They cut open his chest wall and removed his heart. An eyewitness wrote that his heart was huge, and as red as a ruby. Camillus was canonized in 1746, and a large statue of him adorns a niche in the central nave of St. Peter's Basilica.

Along with Saint John of God, who was also a soldier, Saint Camillus is the patron saint of hospitals and the sick. Just a few hundred feet from the tourist hordes crushing to enter the Pantheon in the heart of Rome, the modestly sized but luxurious baroque church of Saint Mary Magdalene fronts a small piazza. Inside, usually alone, and resting in peace, are the remains of Saint Camillus de Lellis.

Saint Camillus, you knew the rough life of the soldier, gambler, and wanderer. Because of your experiences, you practiced great empathy for the outcast, the sick, and the dying. Help us to be like you, to translate our empathy into action, and to be motivated primarily by love of God.

July 15: Saint Bonaventure, Bishop and Doctor
1221–1274
Memorial; Liturgical Color: White
Patron Saint of those with intestinal problems

He seemed to have escaped the curse of Adam's sin

The scholarly heft of Saint Bonaventure legitimized the eccentric Saint Francis of Assisi. Saint Bonaventure was to the Franciscans what Thomas Aquinas was to the Dominicans. These contemporaries form twin summits of scholastic thought, first-rate intellectuals whose eminent writings lent their young, revolutionary religious orders credibility. Aquinas and Bonaventure received their doctorates on the very same day and are shown as equals in Raphael's *Disputation of the Holy Sacrament*. Both Thomas and Bonaventure were also pious, poor, humble, and holy, giving their theological work even greater weight. Saint Bonaventure was part of that huge influx of second-generation Franciscans who never knew their founder. He joined the order in 1243, received his doctorate in theology from the University of Paris, and became master of the Franciscan school at Paris in 1253. In 1257 he was elected minister general of the entire Franciscan order. He was just thirty-six years old.

The pressing responsibilities of religious leadership constrained Bonaventure from total dedication to the life of the mind. He had limited time to read, write, and do research once he was elected head of his order, making the first half of his life his most prolific period of scholarship. But that scholarship was so comprehensive as to be a complete system of thought. He wrote on everything—fundamental theology, the nature of dogma, Scripture and history, the gifts of the Holy Spirit, angels, creation, the virtues—and all of it was suffused with a mature spirituality focused on the individual soul progressing toward God. With this intensely spiritual focus, Bonaventure is said to be more Augustinian in his theology than Aquinas, who is more Aristotelian. The former's goal was to love, the latter's to speculate and to know. Bonaventure's writings on dogma were influential at the Council of Trent and continue to be read.

St. Bonaventure
Cavazzola

Bonaventure led his order in a period of sharp tension among Franciscans over the legacy of Saint Francis. Should the order own property directly or just use property owned by others? Should the brothers be educated and teach or remain simple and only preach? Should the brothers live in the growing cities of the medieval world or stay in the country like Francis himself? Should the brothers in Northern Europe be allowed to wear shoes or must they go barefoot like Saint Francis commanded? These, and many other questions, cleaved the body Franciscan. Many of the diverse interpretations of Francis' legacy were unresolvable, and, in the early sixteenth century, the order morphed into three entities, each embodying a particular spiritual emphasis.

Saint Bonaventure navigated these sharp tensions with great skill. His erudition, great patience, and love of others sewed the diverse patches of Franciscanism into a whole cloth. He had to chastise, punish, and correct too. But he was outstanding in listening to every side before making his final decisions. That Franciscanism survived is thanks to today's saint, who has been called the Franciscans' "Second Founder."

In 1273 Bonaventure was made a cardinal bishop by the pope. Knowing of this Franciscan's humility and his refusal to accept a previous episcopal appointment, the pope inserted into his bull an order that Bonaventure could not decline the honor. Bonaventure was in the kitchen washing dishes when the papal envoys arrived with the news. Saint Bonaventure died with his boots on, while participating in and aiding the pope at the Council of Lyon in 1274. Aquinas had died on the way to the same Council. Bonaventure was buried in Lyon, canonized in 1482, and declared a Doctor of the Church in 1557. Unfortunately, his tomb was desecrated by French Protestants and revolutionaries in later centuries, and his body has been permanently lost. His first professor at Paris, Alexander of Hales, gave him a supreme compliment. He said that Bonaventure "seemed to have escaped the curse of Adam's sin."

Saint Bonaventure, you had few equals in knowledge, love, prayer, and virtue. Through your heavenly intercession, help all Catholics to progress toward union with God by the many paths you yourself walked so long before us.

JULY

July 16: Our Lady of Mount Carmel

Optional Memorial; Liturgical Color: White
Patroness of the Carmelites, and for deliverance from Purgatory

A Crusader legacy enriches the Church's inner life

A few miles from Lebanon near Haifa, a large city in the north of present-day Israel, is the Holy Land's Masada of Catholic prayer and spirituality. Mount Carmel rises high into the sky, dominating the landscape below. On this promontory, one of the most dramatic and memorable scenes of the Old Testament unfolded.

In the ninth century before Christ, the prophet Elijah made a death challenge to hundreds of pagan prophets to determine if the God of the Jews was greater than Baal. Two altars are built. Wood is laid about both. Two oxen are slaughtered and placed on the altars. The pagans pray to Baal to accept their sacrifice. Nothing. They pray through the morning. Nothing. They pray through the afternoon. Elijah mocks them. They hop around the altar. They slice their skin, mixing their blood with that of the oxen. Still nothing. They move to the side. Elijah steps up and gives commands. Yahweh's altar is drenched with water. It is drenched twice more. Elijah pleads that Yahweh accept the sacrifice. And then...a ball of fire cuts through the night sky and BAM! The water evaporates and the sacrifice is totally consumed by the blazing fire of the true God. Then the shocking revenge. Elijah slits the throats of the four hundred and fifty prophets of Baal at a brook that soon runs red.

God showed His power in stunning fashion on Mount Carmel centuries before Christ ever walked the earth. Two millennia later, the Holy Land was Crusader territory. Chivalric Orders of Knights had conquered Jerusalem and dotted the Mediterranean Coast with Crusader castles to protect the flow of pilgrims and soldiers to and from the holiest sites of Christianity. Some of those knights and dames knew Mount Carmel was holy ground. So in the crags, folds, and valleys of this isolated mountainscape, pocked with numerous caves and grottoes, hermits retreated to lead lives of prayer, fasting, and penance. When political and social realities changed by the end of the thirteenth century, and Christians once again lost the Holy Land, these hermits returned home and established new "Mount

JULY

Carmels" throughout Europe, evoking the spiritual isolation of their lost mountain in Northern Israel.

The Order of Mount Carmel is an engine room of prayer, a religious family of both male and female contemplative religious. Carmelites' radical dedication to contemplative prayer, detachment, poverty, and death to self has attracted and formed men and women of the greatest holiness: Saints Teresa of Ávila, John of the Cross, Thérèse of Lisieux, and Teresa Benedicta of the Cross (Edith Stein). Integral to Carmelite spirituality is the Virgin Mary under the title of Our Lady of Mount Carmel.

The origins of today's liturgical feast are somewhat unclear, but the underlying devotion is not. The Virgin Mary's steady, quiet presence in the life of our Lord is notable for its subtlety. Her inner life and secret generosity is what attracts, more than her actions or speech. No word is limited to a book. The Word of God existed from eternity in the Trinity, became flesh, taught, performed miracles, died and rose long before the Word was written down. Mary is the mother of that rich Word. Her word of "Yes" to the Archangel Gabriel gave space for the Word to dwell among us.

In his 1994 book "Crossing the Threshold of Hope," Pope Saint John Paul II wrote that "Carmelite mysticism begins at the point where the reflections of Buddha end…" The goal of spirituality is not merely to renounce the evil world but to unite the soul to the personal God of Jesus Christ. Purification and detachment are not ends in themselves. They help one cling to God more easily. Our Lady of Mount Carmel is not a chameleon. She doesn't change colors to satisfy any and all "spiritualities." She is the mother of God and the icon, *par excellence*, of the queen of the virtues—humility.

Our Lady of Mount Carmel, through your example of humble docility to the will of God, we seek your intercession to make us more prayerful, more detached, more recollected, and more committed to whatever God asks of us.

JULY

July 20: Saint Apollinaris, Bishop and Martyr
First or Second Century
Optional Memorial; Liturgical Color: Red
Patron Saint of Ravenna, Italy, and invoked against gout and epilepsy

An elusive early bishop's memory is preserved in art

Ravenna, a city on Italy's eastern Adriatic Coast, is a miniature Istanbul. It has perhaps the most impressive groupings of Byzantine churches and mosaics outside of the former Constantinople. In the centuries after the Western Roman Empire declined, Italy was ruled by various Northern tribes. The Roman Empire was thus reduced to its eastern half in today's Greece, Turkey, and Syria. Its capital was Constantinople, and its westernmost outpost, and only secure toehold on the Italian peninsula, was Ravenna.

Ravenna's art and architecture, then, reflect Eastern styles rather than Western ones. And it was in Ravenna where today's saint, Apollinaris, was bishop for twenty-six years, and where two basilicas with impressive artistic and historical pedigrees still bear Apollinaris' name. These two permanent proofs of his significance date from the sixth century and, together with an almost equally ancient church in Rome dedicated to his honor, testify to Apollinaris' legacy in the early Church.

The life of Apollinaris is the subject of conjecture more than analysis. Very little is known about him. Some traditions hold that he was a disciple of Saint Peter and came from Antioch, where Saint Peter was the first bishop. Other traditions, based on some historical evidence about the sequence of bishops in Ravenna, assert that he was bishop there in the late second century. Some legends speak of him as a martyr, while others say he suffered for the faith in the manner of a confessor but was not a blood martyr. Owing to these conflicting histories, and to his apparent lack of universal significance, Saint Apollinaris was removed from the sanctoral calendar in 1969 as part of the liturgical reforms after the Second Vatican Council. There was never any question, however, of removing him from the Church's official roster of saints. After a long absence, the 2002 edition of the Roman Missal restored the Optional Memorial of Saint Apollinaris.

JULY

In the older of the two churches of Saint Apollinaris in Ravenna, an ancient mosaic communicates the essentials. The mosaic is not peripherally located. It is front and center in the main apse, in the direct field of vision of any and all who walk through the doors of the church. It shows a man with white hair. He is old. His skull is shaved. It is the tonsure, showing his religious dedication. A large golden halo circles his head. He is a saint. He is wearing liturgical vestments—a chasuble and stole. He is a priest or bishop. His arms are wide open in what is called the *orans*, or praying, position so common to early Christian frescoes and mosaics. He is saying Mass. He is wearing a pallium, a small band of white lamb's wool worn by Metropolitan Archbishops. He is the Archbishop of Ravenna.

Twelve lambs, representing the faithful, look to the figure from both sides. He is an important pastor, a shepherd. His main garment is a white alb. In keeping with the mosaic's age, and with Ravenna's status as an imperial city, the alb looks more like a flowing Roman toga. The empire is alive and well. The figure is an equal to all the powerful of the city. Above the figure, tiny, dark stones spell out: +SANTUS APOLENARIS.

Most of the church's mosaics were wantonly destroyed, likely by the soldiers of a neighboring city, in the fifteenth century. But not this mosaic. It was famous then and is famous now. It is the most tangible evidence imaginable of the importance of today's saint, an early bishop who suffered for a revolutionary new faith that knew about conquering death.

Saint Apollinaris, we know little about you except what is most important. You were ordained to participate in the fullness of the priesthood of Christ. You gave witness to the faith that your people remembered and memorialized. May we lead lives that are equally deserving of honor and commemoration.

JULY

July 21: Saint Lawrence of Brindisi, Priest and Doctor
1559–1619
Optional Memorial; Liturgical Color: White
Patron Saint of Brindisi, Italy

A little-known Doctor of the Church did it all and did it well

Julius Caesar Russo was born into a religious family, yet from a young age was drawn to join another religious family—that of Saint Francis of Assisi. After his father's early death, little Julius was placed in the care of the Friars Minor by his mother. Upon moving to Venice, though, he came to know the Capuchins, another expression of Franciscanism, and joined their Order as a teenager. He took the religious name of Lawrence, was ordained a priest in 1582, and from that point on plowed his way through life like a high speed train. Father Lawrence bulleted north and south, east and west, stopping in Italy, Germany, Austria, Hungary, France, Bohemia, Spain, and Portugal. This one-man army seemed to be everywhere, doing everything, and yet always made the salvation of his own soul his highest priority.

Father Lawrence was smart. Very smart. His intellectual gifts were fully deployed in the service of the Lord to master whatever discipline he studied. He learned the biblical languages of Greek, Hebrew, Latin, and Syriac. In addition to his native Italian, he also spoke Spanish and German, which he put to extensive use in his ministry in Central Europe. His knowledge of Scripture was so wide and so deep that it seemed he had memorized the entire Bible. He even earned the esteem of Jewish scholars for his profound understanding of rabbinic texts.

Lawrence also cultivated a burning love for Jesus Christ, the Virgin Mary, and the Holy Eucharist in long hours of prayer. It sometimes took hours for him to say Mass. He seemed to be carried away in ecstasy and had the gift of tears. This level of fervor, education, poverty, intelligence, and devotion to the Church made Saint Lawrence of Brindisi the ideal priest for his time and place. He was many things, but among them he was the ultimate Counter-Reformation warrior.

JULY

Saint Lawrence explained with great force and lucidity the truths of the Catholic faith to those who had fallen into the trap of Protestantism. He calmly elaborated upon the Scriptural and patristic foundations of the Papacy, Bishops, Mary, and the Sacraments. Lawrence was the anti-Luther and the epitome of the great Capuchins who invigorated Franciscanism in the 1500s and beyond. Amid all of his labors as a preacher and teacher, Lawrence also carried out a parallel set of demanding duties in the administration of the Capuchin Order. He was a novice master, provincial, and minister general, or head, of the Order. Father Lawrence completed mountains of work, day in and day out, for many years, a sustained drive and competence which inevitably led to him being burdened with still more weighty responsibilities.

St. Lawrence of Brindisi leading the battle charge agains the Turks

As a Franciscan dedicated to preserving and restoring peace, Lawrence was tasked by both the Holy Father and secular princes with various diplomatic missions geared toward settling controversies among Christian states and between these states and the surging Ottoman Empire. Yet Lawrence's desire for peace was not divorced from truth, from the right to self-defense, or from love of Christian Europe.

He was the chaplain of a Christian army which was mustered in Germany against the Turks at Lawrence's insistence. Lawrence then personally led the troops into battle with his crucifix held high. The German army's victory was attributed to our saint's intercession and inspiring example. Saint Lawrence died on his birthday, July 22, at age sixty, while on a diplomatic mission to Lisbon, Portugal. He is buried in a monastery in Northern Spain and was canonized in 1881. In 1959 Pope Saint John XXIII proclaimed Saint Lawrence of Brindisi an Apostolic Doctor of the Church for his creative yet orthodox writings on the Virgin Mary and for his commanding erudition in, and harmonious presentation of, Scripture, patristics, and fundamental theology. He is the third Franciscan Doctor of the Church, along with Saints Bonaventure and Anthony, and, unfortunately, one of the least well known.

Saint Lawrence, you were ideally suited to the needs of your age and moved all you met through your virtuous example, vast knowledge, and life of prayer. Through your intercession, help all priests, especially Franciscans, to not spare themselves but to emulate your zeal.

July 22: Saint Mary Magdalene
First Century
Feast; Liturgical Color: White
Patron Saint of perfumers, converts, and hairdressers

An Apostle to the Apostles first spreads the Good News

"Cherchez la femme" is a French phrase meaning "Look for the woman." It is used as a convenient shortcut in movie or literary criticism to discover what is driving a plot, especially in a detective story. Why did the man risk his life? *Cherchez la femme?* Who had a motive to lie? *Cherchez la femme?* Where is the treasure buried? *Cherchez la femme?* It's a cliché, of course, but clichés often convey some truth. Look for the women in the Gospels, and you will not be disappointed. Search for one woman in particular, Mary Magdalene, and you will find yourself present at all the most important Gospel events: the passion, the crucifixion, the burial, and in a garden for the resurrection, just moments after a huge stone is rolled away from a tomb, allowing the Lord to step forth into a new world. Saint Mary Magdalene is present at key moments, says key things, and is a key witness. She opens the door to Gospel scenes that would otherwise remain hidden from view.

Saint Mary Magdalene was among that troop of women who congregated on the outer edge of the twelve Apostles. These were probably women of means, who "provided for" Jesus and the

JULY

Apostles "out of their resources" (Lk 8:3). When these women are named, Mary Magdalene is always named first, similar to Saint Peter's position in the listing of the Apostles. Mary Magdalene is named many more times in the Gospels than most of the Apostles themselves, signaling her importance. The Gospel of Luke relates that seven demons were driven from her (Lk. 8:2). But there is debate over whether Mary Magdalene is also the sinful woman who anoints Christ's feet and if she is also Mary of Bethany, the sister of Martha and Lazarus. Building on the presumption that the sinful woman was Mary Magdalene, medieval traditions wrongly described her as a repentant prostitute. Artistic depictions almost universally show her as sultry, forlorn, and repentant. Despite the dubious connection between Mary Magdalene and prostitution, this association continues today and will likely take centuries to purify.

A "combined Mary" understanding rolls all three of the above Marys—the woman from whom demons were expelled, the repentant sinner, the sister of Lazarus—into the one person of Mary Magdalene. Mary was an extremely common Jewish name. It requires, then, careful attention to the text to sift which Mary is doing what in the New Testament. Magdala was a town on the Sea of Galilee. So when Mary from Magdala is referenced, the reader can trust that her town is adjoined to her name on purpose to distinguish her from other Marys.

An old Christian tradition calls Mary Magdalene the "Apostle to the Apostles." The resurrected Christ appeared to her first, before all others. She is the proto-witness. Mary and other women go to the tomb of Jesus to anoint His body. They see the stone rolled away and enter. The body is not there. An angel tells them to not be afraid, "But go, tell his disciples and Peter" (Mk 16:7), so Mary dutifully fulfills his angelic orders. It is a woman, then, who tells the men, who spreads the news of all news to everyone else. The men come running and verify her account. The tomb is empty. As usual, Mary respectfully remains on the fringe of the Apostles. She weeps outside the tomb while Peter and John are inside. Time passes as they try to absorb what this all means until, finally, the "disciples returned to their homes" (Jn 20:10). But Mary does not go home.

ST. MARY MAGDALENE
July 22

"The twelve were with him, as well as some women who had been cured of evil spirits and infirmities: Mary, called Magdalene, from whom seven demons had gone out,... and many others, who provided for them out of their resources."

– Luke 8:1-3

And then it happens. Mary is alone again, crying. She just can't believe it. She has to take another look. So she bends her body in half to peer into the low empty tomb once again. When she straightens up, she notices a man standing just behind her. She thinks he is a gardener. A short, awkward conversation follows and then abruptly concludes: "Mary!"..."Rabbouni!" (Jn 20:16). Her name is in the mouth of God! A name is enunciated and a new life begins! At Baptism. At Confirmation. At religious vows. May we all hear the voice of the risen Christ speak our name, directly to us, just as Mary Magdalene did, when we hopefully walk for the first time in the garden of paradise: "Ashley!" "Susan!" "Tom!" "Marty!" "Quinn!" "Juliette!"...and on and on and on until the end of time.

Saint Mary Magdalene, assist all who seek your intercession to be humble followers of Christ, doing, from the margins, what is necessary to carry forward the ministry of Christ's Church, quietly accomplishing God's will without recognition except for its eternal reward.

July 23: Saint Bridget of Sweden, Religious
1303–1373
Optional Memorial; Liturgical Color: White
Patron Saint of Europe, Sweden, and widows

A royal widow's visions awe the masses

Upon entering the baroque Basilica of Saint John Lateran in Rome, on the first pillar to the right, is a fragment of a medieval fresco by the master Giotto. It is incongruous with the style of the rest of the often restored Basilica. The fresco has been preserved, partial but unchanged, because of its historical importance. It depicts Pope Boniface VIII proclaiming the first Jubilee Year in 1300. That Jubilee, and its indulgences, brought so many pilgrims to Rome that the original intention to celebrate a Jubilee every one hundred years was reduced to every fifty years. 1350, then, saw the second great Jubilee. Ironically, the Pope was living in Avignon at the time. For political reasons, he was unable to visit the eternal city during the very Jubilee he had called.

Among the throngs of pilgrims who did swamp Rome in 1350, however, was today's saint. Saint Bridget made the grueling journey from far away Sweden. Unlike a typical pilgrim, however, she did not return home after earning her indulgence. Rome became her new home and the platform that made her, and her writings, famous. Bridget only returned to her birthplace twenty-three years later, when her daughter Catherine, also a canonized saint, carried her mother's remains triumphantly back to Sweden. They rest today in a secular museum which, before the Reformation, had been the first monastery Bridget founded.

The details of the first half of the life of Saint Bridget of Sweden evoke a place long lost to history—Catholic Scandinavia. For hundreds of years, the true faith thrived in these lands and incubated great saints such as Bridget. She was married at the age of thirteen and lived happily with her husband for twenty-eight years, bearing eight children. They were a pious couple, even completing the famous pilgrimage to the Shrine of Santiago de Compostela in Spain. But her husband died while Bridget was only halfway through her life's journey. Bridget then spent three years in mourning in a Cistercian monastery. During this period, the spiritual visions she had experienced throughout her life increased in number and vivacity.

After a particularly powerful vision in 1346, she founded the monastery that would eventually be her burial place. But it wasn't built to house an existing order. Responding to the words of Jesus, Bridget wanted to reform monastic life by founding a new congregation, the Order of the Most Holy Savior, or the Bridgettines. The Rule for the new Order was revealed to her throughout numerous and detailed visions. The Order was based on the Rule of Saint Benedict and was approved by the Pope only near the end of Bridget's life. The Bridgettine Order spread throughout Europe and is found in numerous countries today, due largely to its founder's incredible spiritual visions.

Saint Bridget, like Saint Catherine of Siena, labored to convince the popes to return to Rome from Avignon. She invoked the Lord's opinions about the papal exile as He expressed them in her visions. One letter she wrote to the pope was so strongly worded that her envoy refused to read it when he was in the Holy Father's presence. An Italian woman Bridget had become friends with during the Jubilee of 1350 donated a large palace in central Rome to Bridget. Saint Bridget and her sisters established their Roman foundation in that centrally located palace, and within its walls Saint Bridget died. A Bridgettine convent occupies the very same building today and preserves the founder's rooms, as well as a relic of Bridget and her saintly daughter.

Saint Bridget was canonized eighteen years after her death, in 1391, due to her Christian virtue, her deep and sincere piety, her life of strict poverty and assistance to the poor, her devotion to the Virgin Mary, and her many pilgrimages to the shrines of the saints. She was a saint who loved saints. But she became famous for other reasons—mainly because of her intense, highly detailed, and provocative spiritual revelations. The revelations were written down in both Swedish and Latin, translated into multiple languages, and then diffused throughout Europe. Christ's arresting words on death and judgment, heaven and hell, and right and wrong sparked the imaginations of all who read Saint Bridget's writings. Saint Pope John Paul II named Saint Bridget a co-patron of Europe in 1999.

Saint Bridget, may your example of poverty, devotion, and prayer be an example to all who seek to live a life in Christ, and may your writings fire our imaginations to burn ever hotter and brighter with love of God.

July 24: Saint Sharbel (Charbel) Makhluf, Priest and Hermit
1828–1898
Optional Memorial; Liturgical Color: White
Patron Saint of Lebanon

The purest cedar of Lebanon

Today's memorial was first inserted into the liturgical calendar in the United States in 2004. Prior to that, today's saint was known primarily among the Christians of Lebanon, either in their homeland or in Lebanese diaspora communities outside of the Middle East. The dominant form of Catholicism in Lebanon is the Maronite Church. Maronites are united to the Bishop of Rome. The universal Church is like an umbrella under which are found different rites, or ritual forms of praying. The vast majority of the world's Catholics pertain to the Latin Rite. But millions of other Catholics, fully members of the one, holy, catholic, and apostolic Church, worship using an Eastern, or Middle Eastern, liturgy. To the casual Western observer, this liturgy can seem exotic. The Maronite liturgy, rituals, church customs, and forms of prayer are, however, of ancient origin and enrich an already diverse Church with theological fruit picked from one of Christianity's oldest orchards.

Saint Sharbel, baptized as Youssef (Arabic for Joseph), was one of five children born into a poor family from a remote village in the hills of Lebanon. They were devout Maronite Catholics whose relatives included priests and monks. Youssef shepherded his family's small flock of animals when he was young. Very early on, he displayed a tender devotion to the Virgin Mary and a natural disposition toward prayer. In his early twenties, he left the family home to enter a monastery. In due time he made his religious profession and took the name Sharbel (or Charbel) after a second-century martyr from Antioch, a city not far from Lebanon. He then studied, was ordained a priest in 1859, and returned to his monastery to live as a strictly observant monk practicing austere mortifications. In 1875 he was granted the privilege to live as a hermit in a chapel under his monastery's supervision and care.

And there he stayed—alone, isolated, mortified, poor, reflective, and silent—for the next twenty-three years in Christian "solitary confinement," willingly separating himself from the world so he could more easily attach himself to Christ. He died of a stroke at the age of seventy while saying the Divine Liturgy. He slumped to the floor with the Holy Eucharist still in his hands! Saint Sharbel lived the model life of an Eastern hermit-monk in the ancient tradition of Saint Anthony of the Desert.

Western monasticism is focused on community life and liturgy, common meals and spiritual reading, farming, schools, chant, and hospitality. The Eastern monastic tradition has less engagement with the world, and the monks have less contact with each other. Eastern monasteries are often perched on remote mountaintops. They are inaccessible, unadvertised, and imposing. Their monks are like eagles, proud and alone, dwelling in the heights. Western monasteries, on the contrary, are easily found, open their doors to every visitor, and often flower into schools and universities. Some Benedictine monasteries are even embedded within bustling campuses. The different modes of life, rules, and apostolates of Eastern and Western monasticism are stark.

JULY

Although little known during his lifetime, miracles were attributed to the intercession of Saint Sharbel soon after his death. His body was exhumed and for many decades was found to be incorrupt, although it eventually decomposed. Father Sharbel was never photographed during his lifetime, and only a few monks ever saw him after he entered the monastery. But in May 1950 some Maronite monks from the U.S. visited Father Sharbel's grave on his birthday and took a photo. When the film was developed a mysterious hooded figure with a white beard appeared among them. When shown the photo, some elderly monks from the monastery had no doubt. It was Sharbel. All images of the hermit Sharbel are based on this photo.

Saint Sharbel was beatified by Pope Paul VI in 1965 at a Mass at the conclusion of the Second Vatican Council. And in 1977 he became the first Eastern Christian to be canonized in modern times. Various Lebanese government officials attended the Canonization Mass, along with members of Saint Sharbel's family. At the time, a proud Lebanese-American bishop described the new saint as the "Perfume of Lebanon" and as proof that the Maronite Church "is a living branch of the Catholic Church and is intimately connected with the trunk, who is Christ…" Devotion to Saint Sharbel is widespread in Eastern Christianity. In an unusual but beautiful proof of the universality of the Church, devotion to Saint Sharbel was also brought by Lebanese immigrants to Mexico, where images of the pensive, hooded, mysterious looking saint are ubiquitous, and his intercession constantly sought.

Saint Sharbel, may your serene example of prayer, fasting, and mortification be an inspiration for all who do battle in the spiritual desert, for all who struggle with the sins and temptations offered by the world, the flesh, and the devil. Help us to follow your unique path of holiness.

JULY

July 25: Saint James, Apostle
First Century
Feast; Liturgical Color: White
Patron Saint of Spain, equestrians, and pilgrims

Herod strikes again

The primary legacy of the Twelve Apostles is silence. Yes, their voices are sometimes heard in the Gospels, briefly. Yes, they traveled, evangelized, and built up the Church, discreetly. And yes, they were martyred, save John, though obliquely. Who went exactly where, and did what, is guesswork. When, how, by whom, and where each Apostle died is largely conjecture. Even most of their burial places are uncertain. After the Resurrection and Ascension of Christ, and especially after the martyrdom of Saint Stephen, the Apostles dispersed throughout the deserts and mountains of the Eastern Mediterranean world. They gave their backs to Jerusalem. And as they walked away, their trails were lost, sand filled their footsteps, and history's endless cycles erased their exact tracks. With some few exceptions, most of the valuable details were forgotten. The Apostles are now twelve islands of names in a sea of silence.

Some footprints of today's saint, James the Greater, were preserved by Scripture. James was a member of the Twelve and of the Three; Peter, James, and John were the inner core that formed a shield of fidelity encircling Jesus Christ. James and his brother, John the Evangelist, author of the fourth Gospel, were fishermen who were called from their job on a lake to become fishers of men. It's possible that other men were called before or after James and John, and that these unknown men laughed in Christ's face, thought Him crazy, asked a thousand questions first, or just refused to follow a man they did not know and who offered no assurances. Those who said "No" to Christ are lost to history. Christ's was not an open invitation. He was on a mission and kept walking. There was a moment, and then the moment passed. James and John seized their Christ-moment with both hands and never let go.

Peter, James, and John were in the home of Jairus when his servant was raised from the dead. On Mount Tabor they gazed in awe at the illuminated face of Christ, His translucent skin radiating like the sun. And these three were at Christ's side in the intense stillness of a Thursday evening in the Garden of Gethsemane, providing what consolation their presence could. In the Gospels, Saint James is impetuous and full of character. He was not like vanilla ice cream. Everyone likes vanilla ice cream. James's personality seemed to be more like sandpaper or barbed wire. You felt his roughness. You got hurt if you crossed him. James wanted Christ to rain fire on the Samaritans for their obduracy. He even desired to be seated at Christ's right hand in the Kingdom of God, which led the Lord to prophesy his fidelity unto death.

Saint James
El Greco

Saint James' shocking martyrdom was dutifully recorded by the early Church. Saint Luke's Acts of the Apostles states that "King Herod laid violent hands upon some who belonged to the church. He had James, the brother of John, killed with the sword" (Acts 12:1–2). No other Apostle's martyrdom is recorded in the New Testament. Perhaps he was singled out by Herod because of his fiery temperament. He would not have been one to retract a statement. He and his brother, after all, earned the nickname "Sons of Thunder" from Christ himself (Mk 3:17). And so it was that James probably knelt, his neck resting on a block of wood as his head extended just past it. And then the sword fell, the red blood ran, and the holy crown of martyrdom rested gloriously on a head without a body.

JULY

Saint Ignatius of Antioch, in a letter sent to the Church of Ephesus in about 110 A.D., wrote "The more I see a bishop keeping silent, the greater should be the reverence I have for him." A vast forest grows in total silence. The martyrdom of James was like a large tree crashing to the floor of that forest. His death shook the land. Yet the forest continued growing. And it has been growing now for two thousand years. Like a great, but silent, verdant forest, the Church's growth continues. Thousands of miles from Jerusalem and two thousand years after his death, the silence of this Apostle, as that of all the Apostles, still echoes. Every time a baby is baptized, a Mass is said, or a priest quickly walks through the door of a hospital room to anoint a dying man, the mission of the Church which the Apostles established carries on.

Saint James, you died a shocking and unjust death. May your courageous witness to Christ at the end of your life, and your impetuous generosity toward Him during your life, make all Catholics bold and forthright in their love of the things of God.

July 26: Saints Joachim and Anne
Late First Century B.C.–Early First Century A.D.
Memorial; Liturgical Color: White
Patron Saints of grandparents and of Canada (Anne)

God has a family tree, just like all men

Many parents think their child is perfect. Only two sets of parents were ever right. Saint Mary and Saint Joseph had a child through grace and raised that perfect God-son to adulthood. The parents of Saint Mary conceived their daughter in the normal human fashion but without the stain of original sin. So their daughter was superior to them from the start, yet it had nothing to do with hubris. Today's feast celebrates those humble parents of Mary known to long tradition as Saints Joachim and Anne, though they are unnamed in Scripture. The first mention of Anne and Joachim in the Christian tradition is an apocryphal text from the second century which was judged to be fraudulent by the earliest scripture scholars. The Muslim Quran refers to Saint Anne in Arabic as Hannah, says that she conceived in her old age, expecting a male, but was given a daughter and named her Mary. We honor Saints Anne and Joachim because they reared the perfect child and were grandparents to the Son of God.

It is natural for the Church to exalt the earthly origins of Jesus of Nazareth. It communicates something important—that everyone comes from somewhere and someone, even God. The historical Jesus plants a flag in the ground of a certain place, a certain time, and a certain family. No one is from everywhere. No one is from always. No one is a citizen of the world, really and truly. Everyone has one mom, one dad, and four grandparents.

There is a powerful modern tendency to spiritualize Jesus of Nazareth, to assert that what matters most is *that* He was, not *who* He was or *what* He did. This spiritualizing sees Jesus as the highest human manifestation of an ideal, a concept, or a religious principle, but not necessarily as a real man. Such thinking readily accepts that the divine is in the grand sweep of time, in the universal vagaries expressed by karma, transcendentalism, the chi, the tao, nature, and the dreamcatcher. This approach implicitly sees material reality as a mask, and the natural environment as a curtain that must be pulled to the side to reveal the truer, hidden realities of the spirit-based world that invisibly governs the earth. There are many problems with such a worldview. Most significantly, it rejects, *a priori*, that God would communicate Himself to us in outward, tangible, historical forms.

Christianity is not a pastiche of environmental concerns, emotions, moral truisms, and soft love. The Church is not a big electric blanket that covers the whole world. She doesn't exist to make us feel cozy. God comes to us through the very outward, historical forms of a hierarchical institution, through the water, bread, wine, and oil of the sacraments, through words, events, and people. God can speak to us from the inside, from the spirit, from the quiet of the heart. Yes. But He comes to us primarily, in a manner protected from subjective misinterpretation, in outwardness, in time, and in structures. The Supreme Being not only sustains history, then, He is found at a certain point inside of history. History, for the Christian, doesn't just recede further and further into the past. It is ever present to us because God is ever present to us.

For the salvation of just one single man, there would be no need for a Church, for the incarnation, or for the cross. But no one exists by himself, and so no one can save himself by himself. There is never just one man. Everyone comes from two others. The body implies descent from others in a way a spirit does not. Jesus Christ gave us His Body and Blood in the Holy Eucharist, not a treatise of lofty ideals. He did not hand out Bibles at the Last Supper, look the Apostles in the eyes, and say "Read this in memory of me." When He gives us His body, He gives us the DNA of Mary and Anne and Joachim. We touch God. We eat God. We digest God. God becomes part of us. His body becomes our body. And that Body, that flesh and that blood, came down through His grandparents, Saints Joachim and Anne.

Saints Joachim and Anne, may your quiet, hidden roles in the Divine plan inspire all who do the Church's work behind the scenes and out of view to persevere in supporting the Church's saving mission.

July 29: Saints Martha, Mary, and Lazarus
First Century
Memorial: Liturgical Color: White
Patron Saints of siblings

Jesus, an only child, is attracted to family life

Jesus goes to the home of Zacchaeus to encourage his conversion. He goes to the home of Matthew after the tax collector becomes a disciple. And he goes to other homes to challenge religious elites or to speak strong words of censure. Jesus goes to the home of Saints Martha, Mary, and Lazarus, though, just to linger with close friends. Jesus was an only child and probably enjoyed warm fraternization with these siblings around a fire, some light conversation over a meal, or a mellow roof-top chat as the fiery sun set over the ridge of the Mount of Olives just above them. Bethany, it seems, was Jesus' haunt. God loves families and Jesus Christ gravitated toward, and eagerly shared in, the family life of the siblings Martha, Mary, and Lazarus.

For many centuries, the Church's liturgy taught that the "Mary" of Bethany and the "Mary" of Magdala were one and the same, with the "composite Mary" feast day on July 22. The liturgical reforms after the Second Vatican Council, however, specifically identified the memorial of July 22 as that of Saint Mary Magdalene, leaving unresolved whether she is, or is not, the same person as Mary of Bethany. In 2021 Pope Francis resolved this question, at least liturgically. The memorial of July 29, until 2021 dedicated exclusively to Saint Martha, was expanded to include Mary and Lazarus as well. So the memorials of July 22 (Mary Magdalene) and July 29 celebrate two distinct Marys. Mary of Bethany is *not* Mary of Magdala!

Normal, everyday family life is inherently attractive. The chatter across the dining room table, the squabbles over who forgot to feed the dog, the girls who stand too long in front of the mirror, and the boys who leave the room a mess. The tug and pull of family life can be rough, domestic drama, but it is real drama. It's not a video game. It's not virtual reality. Like moths to a flame, people are drawn to healthy families, especially those who come from broken families. And so they come around — the only child from the house next door, the old woman whose children now live hours away, or the childless couple who wonders what might have been. Jesus came around too.

The celibate Jesus may have wondered what it would have been like to have had a brother and some sisters. He seems to enjoy the hustle and bustle of a busy family home, to have a full-throated laugh when something funny is said. Mary is attentive to Jesus. She knows one man very well, her brother Lazarus. Yet Jesus is not like her brother. Not at all. There is something mysterious and powerful about him, something people whisper about but which no one can explain. Mary is so very honored that He is there, she just sits on the floor nearby and listens intently.

Martha is honored as well, and perhaps embarrassed at the state of the house. She is distracted and worried, in the ageless tradition of women who see their homes as extensions of themselves. So Martha doesn't stop cleaning and fussing, even after her guest arrives. She complains, perhaps lightheartedly, perhaps seriously: "Lord, do you not care that my sister has left me to do all the work by myself? Tell her then to help me." The Lord answers "Martha, Martha, you are worried and distracted by many things; there is need of only one thing. Mary has chosen the better part, which will not be taken away from her." It is a woman's duty to worry. It's a way of expressing concern and empathy. She worries about the kids, the house, the food, the family schedule, etc., because if she doesn't worry about these things, no one else will. Jesus reminds Martha, though, that worrying and distraction have limits.

On another occasion, it was not an untidy home compelling Martha to speak. Lazarus has died. Jesus is moved at the news and comes from afar to console the family. Martha goes out to meet him: "Lord, if you had been here, my brother would not have died." The ensuing conversation is compact, powerful, and saturated with faith. "Yes, Lord," Martha says, foreshadowing the promises at Baptism, "I believe that you are the Christ, the Son of God, who was to come into the world."

After Jesus resuscitated their brother from the dead, Martha and Mary were fundamentally changed. Lazarus had been cold to the touch, dead and wrapped like a mummy for four days. And then the sisters held his warm hand in their warm hands once again. Skin on skin - their brother was alive! And the good sisters undoubtedly asked Lazarus, as everyone surely asked him, what it had been like to be dead. Lazarus eventually died again...and was not resuscitated a second time. This family of Bethany followed together the lone man among men who rose Himself from the dead...and who never died again.

Saints Martha, Mary, and Lazarus, your family life of faith provides a model of unity to all siblings. May all brothers and sisters rise above mundane family tensions and disagreements and unite around things eternal and transcendent. Amen.

July 30: Saint Peter Chrysologus, Bishop and Doctor
c. 380–c. 450
Optional Memorial; Liturgical Color: White
Patron Saint of Imola, Italy, invoked against fever and mad dogs

A golden tongued bishop preaches to a golden city

In 330 A.D., the Emperor Constantine transferred his capital from Rome to a newly constructed city he named after himself in present day Turkey. The Roman Empire and its ancient traditions continued but under a new guise. The Empire slowly oriented itself toward Greek, not Western, art and culture; adopted Orthodoxy, not Catholicism, as its religion; and communicated in the Greek, not the Latin, language. Contantinople's walls were finally breached in 1453 by the Ottoman Turks, bringing a definitive end to Byzantium, or the Eastern Roman Empire, after more than a millennium. Due to the capital's transfer in the fourth century, Italy was in disarray at the time of today's saint in the fifth century. Weeds pushed through the cracked marble of Rome's ruined temples. The Western emperors, more warlords than kings, migrated back and forth throughout the 400s between disintegrating Rome and a newly fortified city on the Adriatic Sea. It was imperial Ravenna, Byzantium's sole toehold in Italy. It was a jewel box of a city sparkling with mosaics. Ravenna throughout the 400s and 500s was a mini-Constantinople, Byzantine to its fingertips, basking in the glow of imperial splendor, and abuzz with the construction of palaces, churches, and mausoleums. And it was of vibrant fifth-century Ravenna that Saint Peter Chrysologus was appointed archbishop in about 425 A.D. He served the city well for the next twenty-five years.

Saint Peter preached his first episcopal homily to the empress and is depicted alongside her and the emperor in a contemporary mosaic, proving Peter mingled with the elites and enjoyed their support. Peter developed a reputation as a skilled preacher. One-hundred-and-seventy-six of his sermons still survive. In later centuries Peter would be given the moniker Chrysologus, the "Golden Worded," in recognition of his oratorical skills. The name may also have been given by Western theologians to purposefully rival the Eastern world's famous Saint John Chrysostom, the "Golden Mouthed."

Apart from his homilies, the only surviving document of Peter's is a letter he wrote to Eutyches, a central figure in the complex, and sometimes vicious, Christological and Marian debates of the fifth century. Peter vigorously supported Pope Saint Leo the Great's teachings on the Incarnation, while Eutyches and others in the East had drifted into monophysitism or versions of it. Monophysitism held that Christ possessed one mixed nature which mingled both human and divine elements. The Council of Chalcedon in 451 would formally adopt Leo's teaching, condemn monophysitism, and teach forever and always that a fully divine nature and a fully human nature dwelled inside the one person of Jesus Christ without confusion, co-mingling, or alteration. This complex reality, called the hypostatic union, is precisely what gives such meaning, color, and richness to all that Christ said and did.

St. Peter Chrysologus

During the burning theological controversies preceding the Council of Chalcedon, just after Pope Saint Leo clarified orthodox teaching on Christ's one person and two natures, Chrysologus wrote his letter to the very confused Eutyches. Concisely and charitably, Chrysologus encouraged the heretic to submit to the Bishop of Rome: "Obediently heed these matters of which the most blessed Pope of the city of Rome has written, because Blessed Peter, who lives and presides in his own See, proffers the truth of faith to those who seek it...we cannot decide upon cases of faith without the harmonious agreement of the Bishop of Rome." Peter's letter proves just how widespread early Christianity knew that the Bishop of Rome was the one hub where all of Christianity's many spokes were joined.

Although much is known of Peter's time and place, both theologically and culturally, few details remain of his life or ministry apart from his sermons. These sermons show rhetorical flair in expounding on the Incarnation, Mary's role in mankind's redemption, and in the need for penance and conversion. Saint Peter's golden words impressed the populace of a golden city for decades. We can assume that our saint lived as elegantly as he preached. Saint Peter Chrysologus was proclaimed a Doctor of the Church in 1729.

May all priests and deacons be graced with your passion, clarity, and eloquence, Saint Peter. Help the faithful who seek the fullness of the Word of God to find Him and aid those who are distracted and apathetic to pay heed to God's interventions in their lives.

July 31: Saint Ignatius of Loyola, Priest
1491–1556
Memorial; Liturgical Color: White
Patron Saint of soldiers, retreats, and the Basque country

A soldier reads, becomes holy, and founds a mighty company

Like so many other male saints, today's saint began his adult life as a knight and soldier. In the service of a local noble, he learned the male sins that armies and royal courts excel in teaching: gambling, fighting, treachery, and womanizing. When courageously defending a fortress in Pamplona, Spain, Ignatius was hit by a cannonball. One leg was shattered and the other badly damaged. A long and painful recovery ensued. During this convalescence, he consciously decided to exchange his service from an earthly to a divine Lord. Yet Ignatius' initial conversion developed, over time, into something far more subtle. As he moved toward the Priesthood, Ignatius engaged in profound reflection on the nature of Christian self-awareness, on prayer, and on what it meant to be radically committed to Christ and the Church.

For all of his worldliness and martial experience, Ignatius' conversion started, ironically, with books. To counter the endless boredom of his recovery, he began to read about Saint Francis of Assisi, Saint Dominic, and other saints. He wondered if he could be like them. And then he wondered, a minute later, if he could court and marry a beautiful woman he desired. And then he was carried away thinking about new military expeditions. And on and on his mind wandered, as most minds do. But then came a spiritual breakthrough.

Ignatius reflected on reflection and thought about his thoughts. He plumbed his own depths, in the tradition of Saint Augustine, and analyzed the "shelf life" and quality of his emotions and mental experiences long after they had passed. He observed that reading the lives of the saints and thinking about earthly adventures were both pleasurable. But as time passed, reflection on holy things did not dissipate, while thoughts of earthly pleasures did. Saint Ignatius' astute spiritual self-reflections spurred him to change the entire trajectory of his life. He wanted permanent happiness. He wanted joy. He repented of his past sins and decided to walk the way of the saints.

Saint Ignatius documented his spiritual progress, eventually publishing his insights in his classic, the *Spiritual Exercises*. Other saints and mystics had previously written sophisticated reflections on the normal objects of Catholic devotion. But Ignatius focused on the subject of prayer—the human person—as well as on the object of prayer—God. The mystery of God was equalled by the mystery of man. Ignatius was an innovator in describing the psychological process of praying, in advocating for a systematic examination of conscience, and in encouraging a planned method of introducing into the imagination specific biblical scenes or other objects of Christian faith for reflection. The *Spiritual Exercises* taught the Christian to profit from himself.

Saint Ignatius had an eventful life of wide travel, study, and apostolic activity after his conversion. His high ideals and creative leadership drew throngs of impressive followers. He chose a military name for his new order—the Company of Jesus. By the time of his death, this Company was widespread and continued its meteoric growth long after his passing to become the preeminent Catholic Order of men in the world. It is not too much to say that the Jesuits saved Europe from Protestantism, evangelized entire countries by themselves, educated the higher classes of many nations for centuries, and taught a Catholic humanism of the highest caliber. "One man and God make an army," a saint once said. Ignatius supplied the soldiers, and God did the rest.

Saint Ignatius, may your method and example of prayer, mortification, and study inspire all modern apostles to make Christ the destination and the path, the end and the means, the way, the truth, and the life.

AUGUST

"...the ever Virgin Mary, having completed the course of her earthly life, was assumed body and soul into heavenly glory."

Pope Pius XII declaring the dogma of the Assumption

The Assumption of Mary – Titian

AUGUST

August 1: Saint Alphonsus Ligouri, Bishop and Doctor
1696–1787
Memorial; Liturgical Color: White
Patron Saint of moral theologians and confessors

A lawyer becomes holy

Today's saint was given the gift of a comprehensive education by his parents from a young age. He finished his university studies with degrees in civil and canon law when he was just sixteen years old. After practicing law for eight years, and declining a marriage arranged by his father, the noble, highly educated, and intelligent Alphonsus made a mistake. A bad mistake. He overlooked a simple matter of fact in a legal proceeding and lost an important case for his client. Alphonsus was crushed by the embarrassment. He had never made such a galling, avoidable, public error before. But this one mistake would redound to the great benefit of the Church. Alphonsus decided to abandon the practice of law and his lust for vanity, wealth, and earthly glory. Shortly afterward, he heard an inner voice speak to him, on two separate occasions, while visiting the deathly ill at a hospital: "Leave the world and give yourself to me." This was the turning point. Alphonsus made a dramatic gesture. He went to a church dedicated to the Virgin Mary, placed his sword on the altar, and petitioned acceptance to a local religious Order.

He was ordained a priest in 1726 and travelled throughout the region of Naples as a missionary, becoming well known as a lion in the pulpit and a lamb in the confessional. In 1732, after forming various friendships with local clergy and convents of nuns, he founded the Congregation of the Most Holy Redeemer. The rest of Alphonsus' long life was spent building up this Order. Like so many nascent Orders, it struggled with internal divisions over its identity, matters of authority, and its specific mission in the Church. These struggles caused our saint no end of spiritual torment, especially after a deep division resulted from an act of forgery and betrayal by one of Alphonsus' closest priest collaborators.

Saint Alphonsus took a personal vow to never waste a moment of time. It showed. He did everything, and he did it well. Amidst all of his duties as a founder and priest, he stole an hour hour here and an

AUGUST

hour there to write a page or two, to dictate a few lines, or to take rough notes on a train of thought that had just crossed his mind. Over time, these stolen hours accumulated, and Alphonsus composed volume after volume on theology and devotion. He became particularly well known as a moral theologian. In that sensitive field of study, he acquired just the right balance. He was clear on the Church's teachings and demanding of its faithful but was not overly rigorous. His razor-thin moral distinctions clarified correct behavior on contentious topics but may seem belabored and overly detailed from a post-modern perspective. Alphonsus was personally scrupulous but aware of it. He never imposed his finely tuned conscience on the morally deaf. A Pontifical University in Rome dedicated to moral theology was founded by the Redemptorists and is named the Alphonsianum in his honor.

Saint Alphonsus was made a bishop, over his objections, when he was sixty-six years old. He brought his typical energy and zeal to his diocesan responsibilities, demanding his priests celebrate Mass with true devotion or not at all. He maintained contact with every class of society as a bishop, no matter how downtrodden, poor, or forgotten a group was. His works on the Blessed Sacrament, the Virgin Mary, and Prayer became widely read. His reflections on the Stations of the Cross are still used in many parishes over two hundred years after his death. Alphonsus was also a talented musician and composed the music and words for a beloved Italian Christmas carol. After a long and holy life, he died at the age of ninety-one, an image of the Virgin Mary resting in his hands.

Saint Alphonsus, may your life of spiritual suffering, writing, dedication to the truth, and apostolic energy provide sufficient witness for all priests and religious to do half as much as you did, laboring without cease for the good of the Church and the world.

AUGUST

August 2: Saint Eusebius of Vercelli, Bishop
Early Fourth Century–371
Optional Memorial; Liturgical Color: White
Patron Saint of Piedmont, Italy

A bishop suffers exile and abuse for his defense of orthodoxy

Eusebius was chosen Bishop of the Northern Italian city of Vercelli by popular acclaim in the 340s, even though he was an immigrant from the island of Sardinia. Twenty years after Eusebius' death, the great Saint Ambrose, bishop of the nearby city of Milan, wrote to the Christians of Vercelli during a period of conflict in their diocese. Saint Ambrose's letter survives and is valuable contemporary evidence of the great esteem in which Saint Eusebius was held by an equally great prelate. Saint Ambrose calls Eusebius "a great man." Eusebius was great because of his close attachment to his city, to his priests, and to correct theology.

Regarding attachment to his city, Bishop Eusebius was the first Christian of Vercelli and acted like it. He gave an impeccable witness of poverty, fasting, and prayer. He did not see himself as the leader of only the Christians under his authority but also of the still numerous pagans in the countryside around Vercelli. As one of the first bishops of Northern Italy whose name is known to history, Eusebius lived early enough to have established the first, most basic structures of the Church. He promoted devotion to Mary in local shrines, founded parishes, and ordained and encouraged priests. He promoted Christian identity as more fundamental than one's earthly identity. Rome will come and go, but the heavenly Jerusalem is forever, and all the baptized are future citizens of that heavenly city.

Regarding attachment to his priests, Eusebius was innovative. He had been deeply influenced by Saint Athanasius' *Life of Saint Anthony* and so emulated that monk's life of detachment amidst the hustle and bustle of urban life. Eusebius gathered his priests around him in a community of life which observed a monastic rule. They prayed, ate, and recreated together. They shared the concerns of their people with each other and made those problems their own, as true pastors do. In living this common life, Eusebius and his priests gave a powerful example of Christian solidarity to the city they led. They also prefigured the various forms of diocesan community life which would proliferate many centuries later in the Church, most notably in the Oratory of Saint Philip Neri.

Regarding attachment to correct theology, Eusebius' life intersected with the intense theological polemics of the fourth century, debates which were often intertwined with Church and imperial politics. Eusebius accepted, in full, the teachings of the Council of Nicea. He defended the Council's wording that Jesus Christ was "consubstantial with the Father." He was in good company in defending this proposition—but not in powerful company. The Emperor Constantius, the son of Constantine, was an Arian, and so held to a simplistic, albeit politically expedient, Christology in conflict with Nicene Christianity. The Emperor demanded that Eusebius and other bishops condemn the great flag-bearer of Nicene orthodoxy, Saint Athanasius. Eusebius refused, stating that Athanasius was innocent of any wrongdoing or error.

For Eusebius, it was more noble to defend the truth than to curry political favor. For his defense of orthodoxy, Eusebius was condemned to a long exile in faraway Palestine, Asia Minor, and Egypt. He was mistreated, imprisoned, and abused by his Arian captors, including by an Arian bishop. Theology in the fourth century was played for keeps, it was a zero-sum game in which whatever one player gained, the other lost.

The political winds shifted in 361 when a new Emperor who cared nothing about Christianity took power. Eusebius' long exile thus ended. He then traveled throughout the Eastern Mediterranean attempting to repair the theological tears in the garment of the Church, with limited success. Upon returning to his beloved Vercelli, Eusebius served another ten years as bishop, his quiet and faithful service leaving no documentary trace, a faithful populace his lasting legacy.

Saint Eusebius, you suffered for the truth, not just spiritually but physically. You endured exile from family, friends, and church rather than capitulate to false teachings. May your example inspire, and your intercession empower, all pastors and teachers to equal bravery.

AUGUST

August 2: Saint Peter Julian Eymard, Priest
1811–1868
Optional Memorial; Liturgical Color: White
Apostle of the Holy Eucharist

The Eucharist was the pearl that shone in his eyes

The great artist Auguste Rodin, who sculpted "The Thinker" and other world-famous pieces, met today's saint in 1862 and joined his Congregation as a lay brother. Rodin was despondent over the death of his sister and wanted to abandon art and dedicate his life to God. Saint Peter Julian Eymard burned like a bonfire for God, but this was one vocation his flames would not consume.

Father Eymard could see Rodin's prodigious talent in an evocative bust Rodin sculpted of the future saint while Rodin was a religious brother. Eymard told Rodin to return to the world to pursue his artistic calling. So while Father Eymard was as apostolic and demanding as any saint, he was also just as wise as any saint. Not every man who felt a vocation truly had one. It was for the superior to discern the validity of the calling. Father Eymard knew this well from personal experience. He had lived at least three priesthoods inside of his one priesthood: as a diocesan priest in a parish, as a religious priest in the Marist Order, and as the founder of the Congregation of the Most Blessed Sacrament.

There was never a time when Peter Julian Eymard did not love Christ in the Blessed Sacrament. At the age of five, he disappeared from home one day. His siblings went in search and found him standing right next to the tabernacle in their local church. When they asked him what he was doing there, little Peter responded, "I am here listening to Jesus." His father did not want Peter to be a priest but a blacksmith. He relented a bit over time and then died prematurely, removing all opposition. Peter was ordained a diocesan priest in 1834 and served in a parish. But he felt a slightly different call within his call and began to seek admission to the Society of Mary, or Marists. His diocesan bishop was reluctant to let Father Peter go. The bishop relented in 1839, writing to the Marist superior that "I have given sufficient proof of my high esteem for the Society of Mary in giving it such a priest."

AUGUST

ST. PETER JULIAN EYMARD
August 2

*"Hear Mass daily; it will prosper the whole day.
All your duties will be performed the better for it,
and your soul will be stronger to bear its daily cross.
The Mass is the most holy act of religion..."*

AUGUST

Father Peter's personal energy, apostolic zeal, and prayerfulness led to his being named a Marist Provincial. He traveled throughout France and became acquainted with nocturnal and perpetual adoration societies. He became expert at preaching about the Eucharist and at directing lay Eucharistic societies. During a Corpus Christi procession in 1845, he had a mystical experience while carrying the Blessed Sacrament. His attraction to the Eucharist became so personal and so intense that he resolved "to preach nothing but Jesus Christ, and Jesus Christ Eucharistic" from then on. Discussions with his superiors about orienting the Marist's more toward a Eucharistic identity were frustrated. It was not their primary charism. On January 21, 1851, at the Shrine of Our Lady of Fourviere overlooking Lyon, Father Eymard received the inspiration to found a new Order dedicated exclusively to the Blessed Sacrament. This third call within his one priestly call would consume the rest of his life.

In 1857 the Society of the Blessed Sacrament was formally established in Paris. One year later, the Servants of the Blessed Sacrament for nuns would be founded. Father Peter and his few companions did not limit their Eucharistic dedication to piety and prayer. They prepared children to receive First Holy Communion, reached out to lapsed Catholics, and promoted frequent reception of Holy Communion for all Catholics. The normal struggles of every young Congregation bedeviled Father Eymard: extreme poverty, atrocious lodgings, lack of vocations, and problems of growth.

Rodin's bust captures the essence of Father Eymard better than any photo. Eymard's mass of hair is out of control, communicating his passionate eccentricity. His gaze is penetrating. He knows the mysteries of God and other secrets of the soul. His thin face, straight nose, and protruding cheekbones say he is a mortified ascetic. And buried in his vest, just over his heart, is a scroll. Only a few words of it can be read. It is a fragment of Emyard's prayer: "O Sacrament Most Holy, O Sacrament Divine, all praise and all thanksgiving be every moment thine." His love of the Eucharist pulsated in sync with his heart, every moment of every day of his fifty-seven years. Our saint is buried in his Congregation's chapel in

Paris. He was canonized in 1962 and in 1995 his Optional Memorial was finally included in the Church's universal sanctoral calendar.

Saint Peter Julian Eymard, your ardent love of the Blessed Sacrament consumed your thoughts, words, preaching, and life. May such a healthy devotion mark all of our lives. May we satisfy Christ's thirst for our presence by not making Him wait too long between our visits.

August 4: Saint John Vianney, Priest
1786–1859
Memorial; Liturgical Color: White
<u>Patron Saint of parish priests</u>

A farmer knows God through prayer, not books, and becomes a holy priest

"Is Mr. Vianney good?" the Vicar General asked. "He is a model of goodness," the seminary official responded. "Very well. Then let him be ordained." And thus the last obstacle was removed from the long and winding path to Holy Orders of John Marie Vianney. Young John had difficulty learning Latin, and all seminary courses were in Latin. He had difficulty, in fact, learning anything. He had received almost no primary school education. His father needed John's rough hands on the plow to work the soil of the family farm. Education was a luxury, and poor families had no such luxuries. Schooling was for others. After deciding to enter the seminary, John had to be privately tutored, was almost compelled to transfer to a less demanding diocese, was in and out of different seminaries, and finally personally interviewed to determine if his simplicity disqualified him from ordination. A man hears a call, but it's the Church that responds "Yes" or "No." The Vicar General—courageously, wisely, and correctly—answered, "Yes." Saint John Vianney, the patron saint of parish priests, was ordained in 1815.

After a brief assignment as Vicar in the parish of a mentor, Father Vianney was made pastor of the parish in Ars, a small, dead-end village of farmers, seemingly dropped in the middle of a remote countryside. It was so tiny that, on his first visit, the new priest couldn't find it without local help. When he first stepped foot in the parish, he dropped to his knees and kissed the ground. Father Vianney's humble, servile gesture was known to Pope Saint John

AUGUST

Paul II, who emulated it on every first visit he made to a country as Pope.

Father Vianney would spend the rest of his life, forty plus years, in Ars, burning his candle at both ends until there was nothing left to be consumed. His big heart enfolded the small town within itself. Father Vianney had a simple pastoral plan. His goal was that every single person in Ars go to Mass every single Sunday. Every. Single. Person. Every. Single. Sunday. To implement his plan, he acquainted himself with everyone, fasted and prayed, taught, and heard multiple hours of confessions every day. And he preached, unremittingly, about the fires of hell. If anyone thought there was no hell, then his sermons would have made no sense, because hell was his constant theme. His personality was not for everyone. He could seem fanatical, rough, and just a bit beyond zealous. But his total commitment, purity of life, and moral strictness were obvious. There was also that special something which only a saint has. Father Vianney had it. Like body language, which everyone can read but no one can explain, holiness surrounded him like an aura.

Crowds of people started coming to Ars just ten years into his time there. The nearest large city, Lyon, added trains to and from Ars to accommodate the crowds. Father Vianney himself was the destination of these pilgrimages, not Ars. Unusual spiritual phenomena added to the mystery. People were physically healed, and Father Vianney could read souls, see into the future, and prophecy. But his greatest gift was his own example of holiness. His pithy wisdom in the confessional was so sought after, the lines seeking his counsel so long, that he was made a prisoner of that sacramental box. Near the end of his life, people grabbed at his cassock to obtain a relic. And the night he finally succumbed to his pastoral burdens and died, the simple faithful stripped the bark from the trees in front of his rectory just to have a small chunk of something the holy man had looked at, or which his shadow had darkened. Father Vianney converted his parish one soul at a time using the perennial tools of the Church: prayer, fasting, the sacraments, and preaching.

Saint John Vianney, may your example of dedication to prayer and the sacraments provide an example of holiness to all parish priests so that they may embody for their parishioners the fundamental spiritual truths of our faith.

AUGUST

August 5: Dedication of the Basilica of Saint Mary Major
Fifth century
Optional Memorial; Liturgical Color: White

A venerable basilica preserves its ancient aura

A house is more than a building. When it personifies the family within, it is a home. Or at least it should be. That an office building contains businesses; a house—a family; a barracks—soldiers; and a hotel—guests, is merely to cite particular instances of the architectural credo that "form follows function." Buildings look like what they do. When they don't, everyone suffers from the incongruities. A modern sports stadium doesn't look like a gothic cathedral, because the two architectural forms have two different functions: to entertain or to worship God. Today's feast commemorates a building, not a person. It is a memorial to the "baptism," or dedication, of one of the oldest churches in Rome dedicated to the Virgin Mary. The Basilica of St. Mary Major (meaning the "greater" or "larger" church of St. Mary) was first built in the 350s, in the decades after the legalization of Christianity in 313, when the Church could finally build big. After the Council of Ephesus' dogmatic definitions on Mary as the God-bearer in 431, the Basilica was restored and rededicated.

Of the four major basilicas in Rome, St. Mary Major most retains the atmosphere, the "feel," of antiquity. The sites of the Basilicas of St. Peter and St. John Lateran are ancient, but the present baroque structures date from the sixteenth through the eighteenth centuries. And the ancient, Paleo-Christian Basilica of St. Paul Outside the Walls burned almost entirely to the ground in 1823. The present structure is an impressive replica, but relatively modern. The fourth-century core of St. Mary Major is, however, intact. It has been embellished, added to, and redecorated over the centuries. Nevertheless, it is to Christian Rome what the Pantheon is to pagan Rome—a complete, entire, and unscathed survivor from a built environment which has otherwise disappeared.

For Catholics, every church is a *Domus Dei*, a house of God. Whether it is full of one thousand souls, or silent and empty, it is a house of God. A church does not just keep one warm when it is cold, or dry when it is wet. A church does not become such only on

AUGUST

Sunday. A church is more than a shelter, just like a home is more than a house. A good church is theology in stone. It reflects the truths it teaches in its very shape, in its steps, in its arches, windows, doors, lighting, marble, statues, mosaics, floors, and altars. Every Catholic church should be able to pass the "deaf test." That is, when a hearing-impaired person enters a church, he or she should be able to easily understand what that church is teaching without hearing a single word from the pulpit or one verse sung from the choir. A religion's hierarchy of truths should be expressed, in a confident and certain manner, by the structure where that religion's faithful gather to worship God. One should understand with the eyes. It is not for the Catholic to "shiver in the barn of the Reformation," as one theologian wrote, and to guess what the building is trying to say.

If God himself were to pull open the immense doors of St. Mary Major, one imagines He would walk down the central nave, look to his His right and to His left, smile, and slowly nod His head in pleasure and agreement. There, in an ornate chapel to the right, is Pope Saint Pius V. "How well he guided the rudder of my ship on earth." There, under the altar, are the bones of Saint Jerome. "Oh cantankerous Jerome, you gave my Church the definitive text of my Word." There, below the high altar, is a relic of the manger of Christ. "And there it all started. Resting in that wood, My Son brought the Old Testament to an end." And on and on and on: saints, popes, the Virgin, the tabernacle, the confessionals, the Stations of the Cross. God the Father would not be a stranger in St. Mary Major. He would feel at home, surrounded by the things, signs, pictures, and emblems of the family life of the Universal Church.

Rome is a small planet of art and beauty. The density of artistic treasures in St. Mary Major, and so many other Roman churches, exercises a gravitational pull drawing all those enamored with God and His beauty toward the sacred core of the eternal city.

Holy Trinity, our worship of You is a matter of justice more than charity. We owe You reverence in the same way a child owes honor to his parents. Our love is inflamed by the sacred beauty of churches where You, Mary, and the saints are honored with such effusions of human genius.

August 6: The Transfiguration of the Lord
First Century
Feast; Liturgical Color: White

A preview of coming attractions, our destination is a person more than a place

It was not a miracle that Jesus Christ transfigured Himself on Mount Tabor before the Apostles. It was a miracle that He maintained His common, earthly appearance for the whole of His life. It was a miracle that His face was not glowing like the sun as He walked the hills and valleys of the Holy Land. Christ's normality, His sustained suppression of His divine radiance, was a miracle of humility, of slavish devotion to His vocation to incarnate, teach, suffer, and die for mankind.

The Christian believes in the resurrection of the body and life everlasting in that body. We believe this because of the appearances of the risen Christ after His resurrection, because of His bodily Ascension into heaven, because the gospels specifically mention the empty tomb, and because of the events of today's feast. The Transfiguration shows the splendor of truth. It is a peek into the life of heaven, where we see that Christ will not shed His human skin. Christ will bring His humanity to heaven and glorify it. This exaltation of flesh and blood is one reason why the Church has such immense respect for the human body.

The Church's understanding is contrasted by two extreme views on its flanks: one overly spiritualizing man, and the other overly materializing him. The religions of the Orient stress the inner life of man to such an extent that they see him as a pure spirit caged in the body, glad to escape the confining carcass at death. From this Oriental perspective, the body is a trap for the soul. On the other flank is the Western materialist view. It sees the body as having priority over the soul to such an extent that physical, sensory experience is the best, and only, path to knowledge. This Western lens sees the body as a sensory sponge meant to soak up as many external experiences—pleasure, music, travel, conversation, food— as possible. If you don't experience something yourself, you can't assess its truth or value. This personalizing of existence reduces all reality to "me" and leads to cultural breakdown.

The Transfiguration
Raphael Santi

But neither an excessively spiritual approach nor an excessively material understanding does the body justice. A balanced understanding of the relationship between the body and soul is a hallmark of traditional Christianity. When Christ reveals His glory, He doesn't point a long, bony finger to a colorful rainbow on the horizon. He doesn't puff His cheeks and blow a strong rush of wind on the Apostles' faces. And He doesn't sit down and start playing soothing melodies on a harp. Christ shows the Apostles the truth by showing them Himself. He shows them His arms and legs and torso and face and hair. It's a real body. Jesus gives us a target to aim for. He shows us that the destination is Himself. We desire heaven because Jesus is there. If He were not there, then heaven would not be heaven. He, not a place, is the true destination.

A mystery is not something we can know nothing about but something we can't know everything about. A comprehensible God would not be God, but an entirely opaque God would also be too remote for us to care. Catholicism's theology of the body has a beautiful equilibrium because our God is knowable and yet mysterious. Food, drink, dancing, smoking, romance, music, and beauty are not sins. The body is good, and God took one Himself as proof of that. But while nature is the source of human operations, a person operates them. So the person prevails over the tools he uses. The body, then, must ultimately be a servant. We are enfleshed souls. In heaven, hopefully, we will be most truly us and have our ideal body. Every man and woman will be transfigured like Christ and radiate the glory of the Trinity in heaven, like a white sheet on the line radiates the sun shining behind it.

Lord of the Transfiguration, Your glorified body gives us hope of the glories to come in heaven, where You will be the destination. May Your glorified body inspire all Christians to live well their body-soul uniqueness on earth until they are perfected in heaven through You.

August 7: Saint Sixtus II, Pope; and Companions, Martyrs
Early Third Century–258
Optional Memorial; Liturgical Color: Red
Patron Saint of Bellegra, Italy

The Pope is murdered in cold blood

The sixth pope was named the "Sixth" or, in Latin, "Sixtus." He reigned from 115–125 A.D. The next Sixtus was today's martyr, who reigned from one August to the next in 257–258. Sixtus II (or Sixth, the Second) is listed in the Roman Canon's select roll call of sainted popes: "Linus, Cletus, Clement, Sixtus, Cornelius, Cyprian..." The preservation of his name in the liturgy is compelling proof of the lasting impact of his bloody witness. After the legalization of Christianity in 313, perhaps two popes were martyred, although various others died unnatural deaths. But throughout the 200s, solid historical evidence proves that more than a dozen popes were assassinated by Roman authorities just for being Christian leaders. Many of their remains were interred in an ornate burial chamber in the catacombs of Saint Callixtus, which was excavated in the 1850s.

Sixtus II succeeded to the Chair of Saint Peter at a difficult time. The on-again, off-again persecutions of the early Church were on-again in the 250s. The Roman Emperors Decius and Valerian sought the blood of Christians not only to try to decapitate the surging Church but also to confiscate the wealth and property of

AUGUST

Christians. The tensions in Church-State relations were no less serious than internal Church tensions tearing at its unity. The persecution of Decius from 250–251 was wicked. Decius' edict required everyone in the empire to sacrifice to a Roman god in the presence of a state official, with a signed *libellus*, or certificate, being issued afterward as proof that the sacrifice had been offered. Many Christians were weak and afraid and so sacrificed to gods they knew didn't exist. Some Christians purchased a *libellus*, some fled to the safety of the countryside, and some refused to sacrifice and were cruelly martyred.

Christians' divergent responses to the persecution—some heroic, some weak, some uncertain—were traumatic for the Church. Many in the African and Asiatic Church said that those who sacrificed (the *lapsi*) must be re-baptized. Pope Stephen I, Sixtus II's predecessor, said that the *lapsi* must only repent to be reconciled with the Church. The theological positions of the two camps were each sincere and hardened over time. There was no easy answer. After Pope Stephen died, it seems that Pope Sixtus II was more diplomatic in seeking reconciliation with the African and Asiatic churches over this controversy, although it would not be theologically resolved until Saint Augustine wrote one hundred and fifty years later.

Sixtus II had to be consecrated as Pope in secret because of the times. In 257, the formerly peaceable Emperor Valerian issued an anti-Christian edict which forbade Christians from assembling in cemeteries. Sixtus avoided persecution for many months. But in early August 258, Valerian got serious. A new edict focused on essential targets. Bishops, priests, and deacons could be put to death without a trial. On August 6, 258, Pope Sixtus II was with his flock, seated and preaching the word of God, probably at Mass, in the catacombs. A small troop of soldiers was on the hunt. The Pope must die. With torches lighting the way, the soldiers scurried through the warren of dark and narrow passageways toward the underground chapel. Perhaps they heard some singing. They acquired their prize soon enough, and the deed was done.

Saint Cyprian, Bishop of Carthage, North Africa, received the news shortly afterward and, before being martyred himself, wrote a letter to his flock: "Valerian has issued an edict to the Senate to the effect that bishops, presbyters, and deacons shall suffer the death penalty without delay…I must also inform you that Sixtus was put to death in a catacomb on the sixth of August, and four deacons with him…Let all our people fix their minds not on death but rather on immortality…knowing that in this contest the soldiers of God and Christ are not slain but rather win their crowns." An inscription placed on Sixtus II's tomb over a hundred years after his death by Pope Saint Damasus, rediscovered in the 1800s, verifies the drama of Sixtus II's last moments. It notes that the shepherd gave his life for his flock. The faithful with Sixtus that fateful day walked up the steps of the catacomb into the daylight totally unharmed, while their pastor lay dead. The companions martyred with Sixtus were the deacons Januarius, Vincentius, Magnus, and Stephanus. The deacons Felicissimus and Agapitus were martyred on the same day, but not with Pope Sixtus.

Pope Saint Sixtus II, you were a servant and a leader; a confident shepherd to a frightened flock; a central actor, not a bystander; a witness to truth, not an outside observer; a light generating others' shadows. You are known because you were courageous. Make us faithful like you.

August 7: Saint Cajetan, Priest
1480–1547
Optional Memorial; Liturgical Color: White
Patron Saint of Argentina, the unemployed, and gamblers

A reformer before his time

Gaetano di Conte di Thiene, today's saint, was born with a silver spoon in his mouth, but he spit it out. His father was a count, his family noblemen, and his status and wealth secure. Gaetano studied theology and law and became a senator of his city-state. When he went to Rome, he rose straight to the top and became a functionary in the curia of Pope Julius II. But he secretly desired more—meaning that he desired less. It was not his calling to use his education, position, and family contacts to rise ever higher in the church and society. He wanted a more intense encounter with God, so when Pope Julius died in 1513, Gaetano resigned his papally appointed office and studied for the priesthood. He was ordained in 1516, in his mid-thirties, a late vocation by the standards of his own time or even today.

After ordination, Father Cajetan returned to Northern Italy, his native land, and joined a confraternity of devout men. The men of the confraternity were from the lower rungs of society, signaling Cajetan's break with his own family's privileged background. He then began a life-time of service to the sick and poor in various hospitals and distinguished himself by caring for the most hopelessly ill patients. Father Cajetan's negative personal experiences of the Church of his era, and of priests specifically, were, unfortunately, common. He was scandalized by the tepid spirituality and lax morals of some clerics and saw the need for an ecclesial cleansing.

Father Cajetan saw exactly, or even more of, what Father Martin Luther saw in the same span of years and in the same exact city—Rome—but Cajetan had a far different reaction than Luther. There was no reason to sever a limb from the body of Mother Church. Cajetan sought to transform, not to rupture. He desired purification, not reformation. A different Cajetan from Italy, an erudite Cardinal but not a saint, would debate Luther in Augsburg at a pivotal point in the early Reformation. Our saint didn't debate the finer points of philosophy and theology like Cardinal Cajetan, although that was certainly needed. Saint Cajetan's response to the need for purification in the Church was to purify himself and to invite other priests to join him.

In 1523 Father Cajetan went to Rome to dedicate himself to the renewal of the clergy along with some like-minded friends. They founded a small Congregation named after Theate, the city where one of the co-founders was a bishop. The four founding members of the Theatines were all well-educated noblemen, including one who would later become Pope Paul IV. In 1524 they exchanged their robes of honor for humble habits and professed vows in St. Peter's Basilica. Their charism was to preach correct doctrine, to care for the sick, to encourage frequent reception of the Sacraments, and to restore love of poverty, knowledge of Scripture, and dignified liturgical practice among priests. The Theatines spread throughout Italy doing pastoral work and serving heroically among the sick. Cajetan also engaged in some creative pastoral ministry late in his life by establishing Christian pawnshops which granted loans to the poor, saving the vulnerable from rapacious money lenders.

Saint Cajetan and the Theatines were eventually eclipsed, however, by the more dynamic Saint Ignatius of Loyola and his powerhouse Order, the Jesuits. Saint Cajetan died disappointed at the lumbering pace of the on-again, off-again Council of Trent. He is among that second tier of lesser known saints of the early sixteenth century who spurred the Church to change by their ardor for God and their lives of high virtue. The Council of Trent would not have gathered except for Cajetan and numerous others like him. Great reformers are really purifiers, and they come before, not after, Councils. Our saint was canonized in 1671, and his Theatine Order continues, although only in pockets.

Saint Cajetan, you gave a powerful witness of moral rectitude and of creative apostolic effort. Inspire all priests to live their sacred callings to the full, to purify themselves before they purify others, and to be absolutely dedicated to the truths of the faith.

August 8: Saint Dominic, Priest
c. 1170–1221
Memorial; Liturgical Color: White
Patron Saint of the Dominican Republic, astronomers, and the falsely accused

A one-man army for God; long practice taught him how to preach the Truth

Today's saint and Saint Francis of Assisi were close contemporaries. They both founded influential religious orders, collaborated with the same popes and cardinals, and were canonized soon after their deaths. Francis remains a rich, technicolor, three-dimensional figure even many centuries after his death. Dominic, on the contrary, is a shadow. Francis jumps off the page. Dominic is found between the lines. No cult of personality developed around Dominic as it did around Francis. Yet whereas Francis was unsuited to leadership and perplexed by organizational necessities, Dominic quietly excelled in every area. Because of Dominic's skills, his well-structured order had none of the grave problems that almost doomed Franciscanism. Dominic's personality retreats behind the hum and whistle of the order that embodied his vision.

Dominic, born in Spain, spent many years dedicated to his university studies before accompanying a local bishop on a royal errand that took them across Europe, including through Southern France. In the city of Toulouse, France, Dominic had his first encounter with the Cathars, a heretical sect of rigorist purists on the margins of Christianity. Dominic would spend the better part of ten years of his short life strategically contemplating and implementing a pastoral plan to bring the Cathars back into the arms of Mother Church.

Dominic concluded very early on in this missionary endeavor that the witness of priests had to be more authentic for them to be effective among the Cathars. No more traveling by horse. No more nice meals. No more inns. No more beds. No more shoes. The priests who went to the Cathars must beg like the Cathar holy men. They must walk, not ride, like the Cathar holy men. They must go barefoot, fast, pray, be humble, wear simple clothes, and live strict chastity and celibacy like the Cathar holy men. Then, and only then, would the Cathars listen to the priests. The Cathars listened to Dominic. He had been practicing these many disciplines rigorously and joyfully for many years. He was the very icon of a holy, authentic priest.

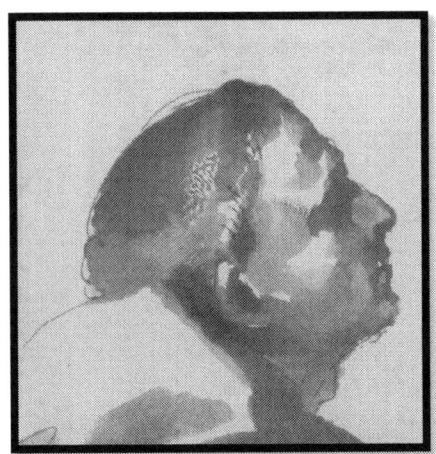

Profile Head of a Monk
Giovanni Barbieri

Dominic, in short, had credibility, and his learning was self-evident in his preaching. Nonetheless, Dominic's pastoral efforts, in the end, had to cede to the religious violence so common to the time. Church and state authorities ran out of patience, and the Cathars were ruthlessly crushed in their vice.

His many years of heading a band of educated preachers amidst a difficult pastoral situation equipped Dominic for leadership and gave him a strong sense of how sound theology impacted pastoral practice. Loving God was not like going on a blind date. The

AUGUST

Church provided the faithful with the tools to know God, not just know about Him. The Church gave the faithful concrete means to love God, not just to talk vaguely about loving Him. Dominic knew the truth and how to present it, by word and example, effectively. By 1215 he had received papal permission to lead his own group of preachers. That same year, he attended the Fourth Lateran Council in Rome to solidify his canonical position.

From 1215 until his death, Dominic traveled, organized, recruited, and planned. He was driving the foundations of his order deep into theological and canonical bedrock. Amidst this tornado of activity, he lived perfect poverty, chastity, obedience, humility, and charity. He was known to often say "Whoever governs the passions is master of the world. We must either rule them, or be ruled by them. It is better to be the hammer than the anvil."

He shared the fruits of his contemplation in every conversation and encouraged his brothers to do the same. His poverty was such that when he died in Bologna, in his early fifties, he lay in someone else's bed, because he didn't have one of his own, and was wearing another man's habit, because his own had crumbled to pieces. The Dominican Order exploded with growth during Dominic's lifetime. It is still today one of the Church's preeminent, and truly global, Orders dedicated to scholarship, preaching, education, publishing, and evangelization. If causes are known by their effects, Saint Dominic was a relentless one-man army for God.

Saint Dominic, your dedication to the truths of the Catholic faith gives beautiful witness to the faithful. Help us to emulate your poverty, charity, and chastity in our daily lives and to strive to obtain your erudition and verve in evangelizing others in our words and deeds.

AUGUST

August 9: Saint Teresa Benedicta of the Cross, Virgin and Martyr
1891–1942
Optional Memorial; Liturgical Color: Red
Co-Patron Saint of Europe

A Jewish intellectual discovers St. Teresa of Ávila, converts, and dies for her race

Edith Stein, today's saint's given name, was a highly cultured European intellectual. She obtained a doctorate in philosophy *summa cum laude* from a German university after being accepted as a student by a renowned philosopher. She mastered numerous languages and worked as both a nurse and interpreter during World War I. She was a naturally gifted and effective teacher. She translated various works of Saint John Henry Newman from English and a work of Saint Thomas Aquinas from the original Latin. She published a book called *Potency and Act* on some foundational concepts in Thomism. Her erudition opened doors to elite circles of artists, philosophers, and other creators of culture. Yet she decided, in the flower of her life, to leave the shore, to wade into the sea of God, and to dive deep for the pearl of great price.

Years after converting to Catholicism, Edith took vows as a Carmelite nun, becoming Teresa Blessed (or "Benedicta") of the Cross. Yet in the convent, her worldly achievements counted little. When she first walked through the doors, one of Mother Superior's initial questions to her was: "Can you sew?" The science of the Cross had begun.

Edith Stein was born and raised a Jew, the last of eleven children in a pious, middle-class German family. But she lost a living faith as a teenager and stopped praying. After passing all of her courses with distinction, and after serving at a war hospital in Austria, she finished a doctorate on the subject of empathy. She then became a full-time assistant to her philosophical mentor. Edith had various positive experiences with individual Christians during the war years. She saw, first hand, how Christians understood their own loss and suffering in light of the Cross of Christ. On a visit to the Cathedral of Frankfurt, these experiences of others' faith merged, rather suddenly, with a profound experience of her own. From the back of the church, Edith saw a woman with a shopping bag enter, kneel in prayer for a few moments, genuflect, and then depart. Our saint was deeply moved by the mystery of it. The woman clearly came into the church to have a short conversation with someone. Edith had never seen anyone do this in a synagogue or in a Protestant church. It struck her—Truth is a person, not a mere concept. God is living, breathing Truth in the person of Jesus Christ.

A couple of years later, in 1921, while spending time at a friend's home, she discovered an autobiography of Saint Teresa of Ávila in the home's library and started reading it. She read all night. She read until the sun came up. In the morning she bought a Catholic Catechism and devoured that too. She had finally found the truth she couldn't quite find in her philosophical studies. She would convert to Catholicism. On January 1, 1922, Edith Stein was baptized. She was confirmed the next month by the local bishop in his private chapel. When she went home to tell her mother that she was now Catholic, the two could only cry in each other's arms at their complex emotions. After her conversion, Edith taught at a Dominican high school, engaged in scholarly work, and lectured on women's issues with the encouragement of her bishop.

Finally, in 1933, after experiencing the dawning anti-semitism of the Third Reich, Edith fulfilled a long-held dream and entered the Carmelite convent in Cologne. Before entering, she went home to say a bittersweet goodbye to her family and attended synagogue one last time with her mother, who felt betrayed and who never responded to any of her daughter's many subsequent letters. Sister Teresa Benedicta took final vows in 1938. On New Year's Eve of that same year, she secretly transferred to a Carmelite convent in the Netherlands to escape Germany's insane anti-semitism. There, she was a model nun, devoted to Saint John of the Cross and to the Carmelite spirituality of the Cross. She prayed in front of the tabernacle for long hours and wrote for many more.

After the Dutch bishops released a letter protesting the deportation of Dutch Jews, the retaliation against the Church was swift and merciless. The gestapo soon pounded on the doors of all local convents to take away any Jewish converts. On August 2, 1942, Edith was praying in the chapel when the gestapo came. She had five minutes to leave. Edith and her sister Rosa, also a convert who was helping in the convent, were taken away. They were transported in trains, like cattle, to Auschwitz, gassed to death, and cremated, most likely on August 9, along with hundreds of other Jews. Edith Stein was sharply aware of her double spiritual identity as a Jew and a Catholic. She knew she was dying, spiritually and physically, for each of her identities. Her iconic life and death, so redolent of the tensions of the twentieth century, caused Saint John Paul II to name her a co-patron of Europe. She was beatified in Cologne in 1987 and canonized in 1998 after a miraculous healing of a little girl in the state of Massachusetts was attributed to her intercession.

Saint Teresa Benedicta of the Cross, you were Jewish by blood, Catholic by baptism, and Carmelite by solemn vows. Your multiple spiritual identities, complex mind, and education found their unity in Christ. May we follow your example in finding our unity in Him as well.

August 10: Saint Lawrence, Deacon and Martyr
c. Early Third Century–258
Feast; Liturgical Color: Red
<u>Patron Saint of deacons, comics, and cooks</u>

A Deacon heads the Church for four days, then perishes like his fellow deacons

The Church's liturgy, like all public rituals whether sacred or secular, is inherently conservative. Its form is not easily altered. Its content shapes, more than is shaped by, the Church and the wider culture. The liturgy moves through time like a great river moves through the land. It plows its own path, carving the terrain, gradually, and incontrovertibly forming a new landscape. One generation is too few to notice, but a few generations pass and, suddenly, a river separates two families, a valley turns into a lake, a dam submerges a city, water destroys what once had been, and the world is different. Feast days and solemnities, most notably Christmas and Easter, shape entire cultures too: their calendars, music, food, festivals, dress, dance, language, art, architecture, and on and on. There is almost nothing that the liturgy and its calendar do not touch. Liturgy creates worlds.

AUGUST

Besides being culture creators, liturgical Feast Days also preserve the past for the present and the future. A Feast Day freezes time and preserves the memory of the world's oldest mind—that of the Catholic Church. The Church does not suffer from Alzheimer's disease. She is rejuvenated with every baptism and so is perpetually young, impervious to the dementia typical of great age. Today's saint, the Deacon Lawrence, is celebrated with a Feast on the Church's calendar, not just a memorial or an optional memorial. This liturgical fact is revelatory and beautiful. He was martyred so long, long ago. He is not Christ, Mary, or a pope. Yet he has a Feast Day! What is the past telling us by this? What is the Church's calendar communicating to the faithful by this interesting fact?

This Feast opens the curtains on the events of August 258 as if they were as fresh as buns right out of the oven. Look and see the cast of characters. Emperor Valerian is to the side, sitting on his marble throne. An official reads the Emperor's decree aloud: "All bishops, priests, and deacons are to be summarily executed." Pope Sixtus II is roughly taken away by Valerian's soldiers during Mass in the candlelight of a catacomb on August 6. Six of Rome's seven deacons are killed with Sixtus. In accord with the Church's theology, they were closer to their bishop than to any priest, so they die with him. The Church has been almost decapitated. There is only one deacon left. The hunt is on for Lawrence, the ranking head of the Church. He is found. He is martyred. It is August 10. The curtain closes.

St. Lawrence
Francisco de Zurbarán

In a tradition already ancient by the third century, Rome had seven deacons to minister to the material needs of the impoverished, widows, and orphans of Rome. Lawrence excelled at this task, which he operated out of a house-church in Central Rome. When the popular and well-loved Lawrence died, he was venerated with a fervor unlike almost any other early martyr. His cult spread like the fire that tradition says roasted him alive. Devotion to him spread as far north as Scandinavia, England, and Germany. Traditions large and small abounded.

The details of his martyrdom are incomplete. But holy legends have supplied what documents could not, and none of them are illogical, mythic, or banal. They might contain the essential facts—he was burned alive on a gridiron. Lawrence was buried just outside the walls of ancient Rome, where a minor basilica, also the burial site of Pope Pius IX, still stands. Numerous other churches in Rome are dedicated to his memory, including the house-church where he ministered. The current church on the site is, to this day, still enclosed inside of a larger building just as the house-church was. The deacon-martyr Lawrence gave a witness so powerful to Rome that his death may have been the no-going-back-moment which proved that Christianity was here to stay, forever, in the capital of the world.

Saint Lawrence, may your example inspire all clergy, and especially deacons, to remain close to both their bishops and their people, providing faithful witness to the truths of our faith, which are worth living and dying for.

August 11: Saint Clare, Virgin
c. 1193–1253
Memorial; Liturgical Color: White
Patron Saint of embroiderers, goldsmiths, and laundry workers

She heard Francis, left comfort, and slept on the floor for forty-one years

Silicon Valley is not, topographically, a valley. The name is a contrivance dating from the 1970s and 80s. The actual valley is named after today's saint. Santa Clara Valley, running southeast from the southern shores of San Francisco Bay, was named after its beating heart, Mission Santa Clara de Asís—a church, school, and farm—founded by Franciscan Friars in 1777. The current mission church, a beautiful twentieth-century idealization of mission architecture, sits on the site of the original Mission structure and is the iconic campus centerpiece of Santa Clara University, California's oldest. It's likely that Saint Clare never left her convent in Assisi, Italy, for the last forty years of her life. Yet a valley, city, and university in far away California are named in her honor. That a medieval, cloistered, Catholic nun is still so present to a hyper-modern portion of the world is a testament to the global reach and cultural impact of Catholicism and the Franciscan order.

Clare of Assisi was born about a decade after and in the same small town as Saint Francis. Many of Clare's earliest friends became nuns in her community, survived her, and gave testimony in her canonization process, reporting interesting details about her early life. Clare was from an economically comfortable family in the upper part of Assisi, in the neighborhood of the nobility. She had two younger sisters. Her mother was pious and had gone on long pilgrimages to holy shrines. Her household included knights and soldiers. From an early age she was interested in religious life and gave religious instruction to the many servants and others in her vast household.

Clare was a prize to her father, as eligible daughters were like pawns whose marriages could seal alliances with other noble families. An Assisi marriage broker testified, after Clare's death, that he had approached Clare various times with offers of marriage from interested suitors. She turned him down each time and instead challenged the broker about the quality of his own Christian commitment. If Clare had never met Saint Francis, she may well have become a Benedictine nun in a convent for noble women, putting her education to good use in the copying of sacred manuscripts.

But she did meet Saint Francis, so her natural religiosity turned more radical. At the age of eighteen, Clare heard Francis preach in a local church and was deeply moved, as so many were, by his presence as much as his words. She began to meet with him privately to talk about the things of God and a new plan for her life. On Palm Sunday in Assisi, there was a tradition that eligible young ladies would process down the aisle of the Cathedral to receive a blessed palm branch from the Bishop's own hands. Interested local bachelors showed up to watch this kind of sacred debutante parade.

AUGUST

Clare was in the Cathedral on Palm Sunday 1212, but she did not process with all the others. Instead, the Bishop, known to history as Guido, descended the sanctuary steps and extended a palm to her as she remained in her pew. Christ would be her spouse. Her plan was about to unfold.

That very night, Palm Sunday 1212, Clare secretly fled her family home and, with Francis' help, entered behind the barred doors of a local convent. She donned a rough habit, and her hair was shorn. The men in her family were alarmed and rushed to bring her home and to her senses. Clare would not budge. As they tried to drag her out of the chapel, she grabbed the altar as an anchor and tore its linens to the floor. The men finally recognized the law of sanctuary and retreated. Clare never deviated from the path she chose that Palm Sunday night. Her close, holy relationship with Francis would endure until his death. He was the leader, the giver, the essential figure. She provided support and allegiance.

Clare would go on to become the first woman to write a rule for other women. She became the foundress of all female Franciscan religious, who number in the tens of thousands today. She had an iron will, a great capacity for physical suffering, and lived a cloistered life of intense and continual prayer. For Clare and her spiritual progeny, the Poor Clares, religion was not primarily an internal disposition. Religion cannot be reduced to mere feelings, pious thoughts, or holy words. It is not a truly great and religious thing to separate the paper from the plastic in the recycle bin. It is a truly great and religious thing to go barefoot, to fast, to abstain from meat, to remain chaste, to wear a coarse habit against the skin, to pray long hours on your knees, to sleep on the floor, and to spend the night shivering in the cold. Such a life is for the few. But there are such few in the world, even today. Of their lives, nothing is counterfeit. Of Saint Clare's life, nothing was counterfeit either.

Saint Clare of Assisi, you chose a radical form of love of God as a cloistered nun. May your example and your prayers inspire all Catholics, especially female religious, to organize their entire lives around God, His Son, and His Church.

AUGUST

August 12: Saint Jane Frances de Chantal, Religious
1572–1641
Optional Memorial; Liturgical Color: White
Patron Saint of widows and parents separated from their children

An aristocratic widow's grief is transformed into love of God

Today's saint was well born and acted like it. She was educated, refined, beautiful, witty, and wealthy. She married a baron, lived in his castle, and together they raised four children. But then tragedy struck like lightning. Her husband was killed in a hunting accident. Jane was a widow at just twenty-eight. She found it nearly impossible to forgive the man who had caused her husband's death. Grief and anger consumed her. But in 1604 she heard a homily that she needed to hear, from a wise, holy bishop who spoke with great erudition, passion, and eloquence. It was the great Saint Francis de Sales on one of his endless tours across Southern France. He was in Dijon, Jane's homeland, and she saw in him the embodiment of the spiritual guide whom God had promised her in a mysterious vision. The two bonded in a holy friendship not unknown among the saints and remained close until de Sales' death.

Jane de Chantal wanted to become a nun, but Francis dissuaded her...for the time being. Once she had provided for her children and taken care of various practical matters, she was finally ready to uproot herself and move to Annecy, near Geneva, Switzerland, to start a Congregation of religious sisters. Her fourteen-year-old son was rightly perplexed at his mother's decision to leave him for God, even though Jane had arranged for the boy to be cared for by Jane's brother, a bishop. In one of history's most poignant, yet humorous, illustrations of Christ's commandment to leave father and mother and wife and children for Him, the boy dramatically blocked his mother's departure for the convent by lying on the floor across the threshold of the door. A priest in the room asked Jane if her son's tears would change her mind. "No," Jane replied, "but still, I am a mother." She cried, and then stepped over her son's supine body, and left. Moved? Yes, definitely. Deterred? No. Not in the least.

Jane Frances de Chantal founded the Congregation of the Visitation in 1610. Its sisters were often women who had been unwelcome in other religious congregations due to illness, age, or the inability to live the strict life of penance and fasting required in most convents. The Visitation nuns' initial active apostolates were eventually curtailed in favor of a cloistered existence based on the traditional rule of Saint Augustine. Saints Francis and Jane prized two virtues in their nuns above all others: humility and gentleness. The Annecy Visitation Convent grew into a magnet for Catholic aristocrats, princes, and princesses attracted to Jane's practical *savoir-faire*, charm, gentility, and holiness.

After the death of Saint Francis de Sales in 1622, Jane destroyed all of the correspondence they had exchanged over the years. They were truly co-founders of the Visitation order and spiritual twins. Incredibly, another spiritual giant, Saint Vincent de Paul, replaced Francis de Sales as Jane's spiritual director. Jane grew in holiness behind the walls of her cloister and developed a reputation as a saint, one which she rejected. After many physical and interior sufferings, she died a holy death, was beatified in 1751, and canonized in 1767. She was indeed rewarded by Christ a hundredfold for having cut ties with her family. There were eighty-six Visitation convents established by the time of Jane's death, and the Order continued to expand after she died. Visitation convents are still present in many countries throughout the world. Saint Jane Frances de Chantal is buried in a sumptuous golden tomb in the Visitandine church in Annecy, just a few feet from the tomb of her holy mentor, Saint Francis de Sales.

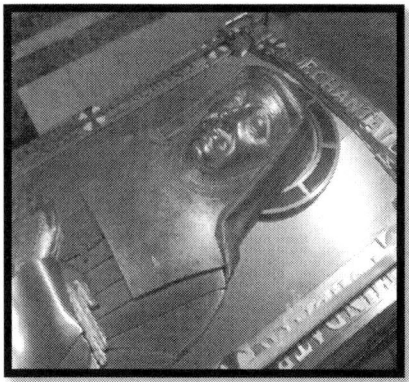

Tomb of St. Jane Frances de Chantal
Annecy, France

Saint Jane Frances de Chantal, your commitment to God grew out of grief over your husband's untimely death. May we convert every sadness, loss, and trial in our lives toward the good, redirecting our hurts into an ever more intense love of God.

AUGUST

August 13: Saints Pontian, Pope; & Hippolytus, Priest: Martyrs
Late Second Century–c. 235
Optional Memorial; Liturgical Color: Red
Patron Saint of Montaldo Scarampi, Italy (Pontian) and prison guards (Hippolytus)

An exiled Pope dies along with a learned priest

Today's martyrs died on the island of Sardinia, perhaps from overwork in the mines or perhaps from starvation or neglect rather than execution. In a pacific interlude following the persecution which was their doom, a later pope, Fabian, returned their bodies to Rome for dignified burial. Pontian was interred in the papal crypt in the Catacombs of Callixtus near so many of his fellow popes of the 200s. In 1909 the original marble epitaph on Pontian's tomb was found among the shards littering the floor of the catacombs. It reads ΠΟΝΤΙΑΝΟC ΕΠΙC ΜΡΤ (Pontian, Bishop, Martyr), although the abbreviation for "martyr" was engraved by a different hand. Tombstones are very economical. Hippolytus was buried in a Roman catacomb, subsequently named in his honor, which became a pilgrimage site. The links among today's martyrs are their common date of burial, August 13, and their place of death. Hippolytus is by far the more significant figure.

Pope Saint Pontian was consecrated Bishop of Rome in 230. He is chiefly known for convening a Roman Synod which confirmed a prior condemnation of the Egyptian theologian Origen. Like so many other bishops of his era, Pontian also dealt with divergent positions over how the Church should re-integrate Christians who had abjured their faith during a persecution. Should they be re-baptized, do public penance, or be welcomed back privately? Tensions over this issue perdured for many decades and deeply wounded Church unity. During a persecution, Pontian was exiled, but first graciously resigned in 235 so that a successor pope could be elected. For this magnanimous act, he was remembered as "distinguished" in contemporary documents.

Saint Hippolytus is an elusive figure. He was most likely from Rome. Some traditions, however, state he was from Lyon and was a disciple of Saint Irenaeus. Incredibly for a saint, Hippolytus is also traditionally labeled an anti-pope for resisting Pope Callixtus' lenient attitude in reintegrating into Church life the *lapsi* who had rendered homage to false gods. Hippolytus was later reconciled to the Church which he loved enough to disrupt. Besides being a controversialist, Hippolytus was the most impactful theologian in Rome before the legalization of Christianity. When the great theologian Origen came to Rome from Caesarea, he heard Hippolytus preach. Most of Hippolytus' works have been lost, but enough translated fragments of his original Greek writings survive to capture his importance. He wrote on Scripture, dogma, law, apologetics, Christ, and also authored a comprehensive polemical work entitled *A Refutation of All Heresies*.

Hippolytus is most famous as the author of the *Apostolic Tradition*, which preserves some of the most ancient liturgical texts of the primitive church. The original of the *Apostolic Tradition* does not exist, and later translated fragments are of dubious provenance, making the work a fluid, composite text of different eras. Nevertheless, the core document is a one-of-a-kind artifact, allowing a modern Christian to peek through the keyhole into the liturgy of the early, praying Church. Hippolytus doesn't just describe the words and actions of the liturgy, as the earlier Didache and Saint Justin Martyr did. Instead, he writes down the actual prayers.

The *Apostolic Tradition* contains the earliest known rite of ordination. The ordination rite of a bishop used today by the Catholic Church still largely adopts this ancient text. Hippolytus provides the first example of the Virgin Mary being invoked in liturgical prayer. And Hippolytus' prayers for the Eucharistic banquet include the third-century words of consecration! This text is the source for a significant portion of today's Eucharistic Prayer II, perhaps the most commonly used Eucharistic prayer at Mass. When the faithful throughout the world hear the familiar cadence of Eucharistic Prayer II each Sunday, they are hearing a distant echo—it's the sound of priestly voices from the third century.

As he did on so many significant Roman tombs, Pope Damasus (366–384) wrote an inscription on the tomb of Hippolytus more than a century after the saint died. Part of it reads: "Wherever he was able to go, he had spoken of the Catholic faith so that all might follow it. Thus our martyr deserves to be acknowledged." Indeed. And at the entrance of the forever-closed catacombs of Saint Hippolytus, a personalized graffiti from an ancient pilgrim is carved into the wall, a tender petition invoking today's saint: "Hippolytus, keep Peter the sinner in mind." Saint Hippolytus, keep all of us in mind.

Saints Hippolytus and Pontian, you lived at a difficult time and gave such public witness that you were exiled when many others were not. Your headship of the Church led to your demise. You were isolated, suffered want, and died as a result. May we count our own hardships little in light of yours.

August 14: Saint Maximilian Mary Kolbe, Priest and Martyr
1894–1941
Memorial; Liturgical Color: Red
Patron Saint of prisoners, drug addicts, journalists, and the pro-life movement

Prisoner 16670 was tough, immersed in God, and ready when the moment came

Saints are made, not born. Even more so martyrs. Maximilian Kolbe was so impressive a man that he may have been canonized even if that oh-so-brief, oh-so-intense, my-life-for-his exchange in the grim prison yard of Auschwitz had not led to his martyrdom. Baptized as Raimund, from a young age Kolbe felt the call to self-sacrificing holiness. When he was a boy of twelve, the Virgin Mary came to him in a vision and held out two crowns for him to choose from: one white for a life of purity, and one red for martyrdom. The preteen Maximilian responded to his Lady: "I choose both."

Maximilian, along with his older brother, entered a local Franciscan seminary as a teen. When he was just eighteen, his superiors sent him to study in Rome, where he earned doctorates in philosophy and theology *summa cum laude*. He was ordained a priest in 1918 and the next year returned to the new, post-World War I country of Poland. For the next twenty plus years, Father Maximilian powered his way through life. He taught in a Franciscan seminary. He started an immense publishing house which printed devotional materials promoting the Army of the Immaculate. He founded a new Franciscan monastery, which rapidly grew into one of the largest in Poland. And in 1930 he became a missionary to the Far East. He went to China, had little success, and so went on to Japan, where he founded a monastery near Nagasaki. He also started a publishing house in India. In 1936 he returned to Poland due to ill health. But he didn't stop. He continued to manage various Marian publications, which were widely circulated, and even procured a radio license and began broadcasting from his own monastery radio station. As he immersed himself in the thousands of details of these varied apostolates, Father Kolbe maintained a disciplined life of prayer, mortification, and daily Mass.

After the Germans invaded Poland in September 1939, Kolbe's apostolates were curtailed. He organized a hospital at the monastery and, along with the reduced community of brothers, gave shelter to refugees, including about 2,000 Jews. He was arrested by the Germans in 1939 and held for almost three months. He was pressured, but refused, to sign a document recognizing his German ancestry (Kolbe's father was an ethnic German) in exchange for more food rations and better treatment. In February 1941, German SS men came and shuttered his monastery. Kolbe and four other friars were arrested, though twenty other brothers offered themselves in their stead. In May 1941, Kolbe was transferred to the heavy labor division of Auschwitz for the last act of his life.

He carried out his priestly ministry as best he could in the hell of Auschwitz and endured severe beatings for it. In July, just two months after he arrived, a prisoner escaped from the camp. As both deterrent and reprisal, the head of the camp ordered ten men to be starved to death in the escapee's place. The victims were chosen at random from a prisoner roll call. One of the unfortunate chosen, a married man named Francis, begged for mercy: "My wife! My children!" What followed this desperate pleading was profound, left an indelible impression on all who witnessed it, and is packed with an almost liturgical character.

Perhaps remembering his childhood vision of the Virgin, and perhaps inspired that the chosen man shared the name Francis with the founder of his religious order, Kolbe removes his cap and slowly emerges from the bedraggled group of prisoners. A filthy, striped rag of a uniform is draped over his skeletal frame. He is barefoot. But he has dignity. There are no frivolous men in Auschwitz. He speaks directly to the commanding officer in German: "I want to take his place." Kolbe's bearing must command respect, because, according to an eye-witness, the officer responds to him using the formal "You." "Warum wollen Sie für ihn sterben?"—"Why do you

Sir want to die for him?" "Because he has a wife and children." "What is your profession?" "I am a Catholic priest." A few moments of silence and then "Gut." "Good" or "Right."

After two weeks of no food or water in a bunker, a guard injected carbolic acid into the arm of the indestructible Kolbe on August 14. His body was cremated the next day. His ashes floated from the smokestack over the gray wasteland of Auschwitz on August 15, the Feast of the Assumption. He, a priest, became what he offered. Like Saint Polycarp of old, burned like bread at the stake, Kolbe's life ended in a liturgical doxology where his own body became the bread of sacrifice.

First-class relics of Saint Maximilian exist only because his Franciscan barbers thought he was a saint. They saved hairs from his head and beard without his knowledge. The man whose life he saved, Francis Gajowniczek, lived for another fifty-three years, to the age of 93, dying in 1995. He was present in Rome when Pope Saint John Paul II, who lived just an hour from Auschwitz in 1941, canonized his fellow Pole Saint Maximilian Kolbe in 1982.

Saint Maximilian Kolbe, you were prepared to be generous in your last moments by a long life of sacrifice, humility, and devotion. May we so prepare ourselves day in and day out, so that when a moment of heroic generosity presents itself, we will respond like you.

August 15: The Assumption of the Blessed Virgin Mary
First Century
Solemnity; Liturgical Color: White
<u>Patron Saint of France and Lebanon</u>

God wants Mary for Himself

Today's Solemnity of the Assumption of Mary body and soul into heaven commemorates, liturgically, a dogma. Catholicism celebrates her dogmas like a country celebrates its independence day or its military victories. The Church processes up and down city streets for the Body and Blood of Christ; she builds crèches and composes Christmas carols for the dogma of the Incarnation at Christmas; she names cities, such as Asunción, the capital of Paraguay, after dogmas such as today's Feast. We strew flowers, sing songs, walk on pilgrimage, construct shrines, and kneel in prayer for our dearest truths. Tradition in the Church is not a locked chest. It is a vital force, like a rushing wind, that purifies and is purified, that is ever ancient and ever young, and that informs all that the Church teaches and does. The sacramental family of the Church celebrates her most deeply held, specifically defined beliefs, or dogmas, in beautiful ways.

The Assumption of Mary into heaven is a logical consequence of the dogma of the Immaculate Conception. Because Mary was born without original sin, she did not suffer its consequences, among which is death. Because she was a kind of Ark of the New Covenant, carrying the Church in the person of Christ, God preserved her from sin and wanted her in His presence when her time on earth ceased. No saint has ever enjoyed such a privilege, because no saint ever had the relationship with Christ that Mary enjoyed. A pious tradition says that the choirs of angels in heaven whispered in awe to each other as Mary was assumed into God's presence, "Who is this woman treated with such unique respect and honor?"

Sometimes it's hard to appreciate the beauty and majesty of a massive landscape without a person to give it scale. How high is that waterfall? How tall that mountain peak? How far that shore? Place a person in the field of vision and suddenly the image makes more sense. God fills every scene with his majesty. He is almost too much to take in. But Mary gives God scale and perspective. She humanizes the view. Mary is always there in the foreground, showing the faithful how to approach God and render Him due honor.

Devotion to the Virgin Mary is not just a more intense version of devotion to a saint. It is so much more than that. True devotion to Mary is on a higher plane of spirituality, something "cradle Catholics" know instinctively, even if they cannot explain it. With Mary as our mother, the Church and her doctrines are vivified. They seem to matter more. The Church is closer to us and we to her because of Mary. Marian spirituality is more than religious wisdom in the Eastern tradition. It is more than acknowledging that Jesus Christ came from a particular woman and a particular town. To be "Marian" is to know why God would want her assumed into heaven, body intact. To be "Marian" is to understand that no one asks about a baby without asking about its mother in the very same breath. Mary was not just the first Christian. She was, for years, the only Christian. She was, for years, the entire Church.

The dogma of the Assumption, like all dogmas, is liberating. Borders make one go deeper, just like irrigation channels guide the water where it's needed so that a harvest will come. "No" can lead to new discoveries as much as "Yes." Good theology sometimes says "No" to bad theology. This usually leads to a deeper spirituality. We need sound mysteries of faith to contemplate, to consider, and to commemorate. Without them, we would be focused either on falsehoods or on ourselves, and we might then become the mystery of faith rather than the truth or God. Profound dogmas of faith such as the Assumption of Mary walk hand in hand with a vibrant spiritually. Mary's Assumption into heaven opens new horizons to the mind and imagination in prayer and a holy desire to discover more in the life to come.

Saint Mary, assumed into heaven, may your life with God, body and soul, be our goal. May we see your quiet devotion to God and the Church as an example to be followed, a target to be aimed at, and a destiny that awaits the serious Christian who emulates your subtle virtues.

August 16: Saint Stephen of Hungary
c. 975–1038
Optional Memorial; Liturgical Color: White
Patron Saint of Hungary and of kings

Baptized by his pagan father, made King by the Pope, his heirs demolished his legacy

Saint Stephen of Hungary was a warrior king whose silhouette stands proud on a far distant horizon as the sun rises behind him at the dawn of the medieval age. His year of birth can only be guessed, as ancient chronicles give conflicting dates. His father was of that generation of rough pagans who had to confront the new, vibrant force of Catholicism which challenged the old ways of paganism and its local gods who satisfied local needs. The Mediterranean Basin had long been Christian by the tenth century. But daring missionaries had only recently penetrated deep into the wide plains of the Magyars, the Bulgars, and that vast land of the Rus that lay beyond. That Christian dawn in Eastern Europe is when our saint first comes on the scene.

He was born Vaik and baptized Stephen when his father, a duke, converted to Christianity. When he was about twenty-two, he succeeded his father as a Magyar leader and warlord. After consolidating his territory and power through various wars, he sent an emissary to the Pope in Rome to petition for the founding of Church structures in his land. Pope Sylvester II concurred with Stephen's plans and took him one step further. Tradition holds that the Pope had a crown fashioned for Stephen and sent it to Hungary, where the papal ambassador crowned Stephen king in 1001.

King Stephen took his duties as a Catholic king with utmost seriousness. He founded an enormous Benedictine monastery, numerous dioceses, and mandated one tax-supported parish with a priest for every ten towns. He built a shrine to the Virgin Mary, which became the sacred forum for the coronations, and burials, of the kings of Hungary. He aggressively punished those who practiced the outlawed pagan customs of yesteryear and prohibited marriages between pagans and Christians. Interestingly, he required that all his subjects be married, except for priests and religious.

After sadly familiar intrigues over succession, money, and power, Stephen died on August 15, 1038. Most of his children had died as infants, and his one adult son, his presumptive heir, died in a hunting accident in 1031. Thus Stephen's efforts to establish a Christian state were placed in jeopardy. Just as Stephen had feared, once the mighty king died, all of his accomplishments were neglected. Chaos and civil war raged for decades after his burial. The two ostensibly pagan kings who succeeded him were apathetic, or even antagonistic, toward Christianity. The fruits of Stephen's Christian efforts rotted on the tree, and his immediate legacy dissipated.

Eventually, order was restored to Hungary, and Stephen's greatness was recognized. He was canonized in 1083. He is now a revered saint-founder of the Hungarian nation. The Huns, the Goths, and the Vandals don't have a nation today. Over time, these pagan tribes

AUGUST

ST. STEPHEN OF HUNGARY
August 16

"My dearest son, if you desire to honor the royal crown, I advise, I counsel, I urge you above all things to maintain the Catholic and Apostolic faith with such diligence and care that you may be an example for all those placed under you by God..."

– From St. Stephen's admonitions to his son Emeric

were absorbed into the stable cultures they invaded. They melted into the many nations and identities of modern Europe. The Magyars, however, did not disappear, merge with other peoples, or melt away. They have their own nation, language, culture, art, and history. They are the people of Hungary, and they owe their enduring identity to Saint Stephen. He imposed the stability of a first-class religion on a horse-riding clan and so transformed that roaming tribe into a stable nation.

Stephen gave his people God. And to God and His Church they were faithful. Hungary matured over the centuries like wine, until it was a refined Christian nation, a defender of Christ and the Church. Neighboring tribes resisted the gospel and dissipated into thin air with the passing of time. Saint Stephen was a model King because he knew that to found a country you have to found a Church along with it.

Saint Stephen, you bear the name of the first martyr of the Church and showed similar courage in battling the enemies of God. May your brave and visionary leadership embolden all civil and church leaders to lay the foundations for a success which flourishes long after they have died.

August 19: Saint John Eudes, Priest
1601–1680
Optional Memorial; Liturgical Color: White
Patron Saint of the Diocese of Baie-Comeau, Québec

His fine education led to a life of deep prayer and identity with Jesus

Many educated Catholics are familiar with the great Spanish saints of the 1500s: Saints Ignatius Loyola, Francis Xavier, John of the Cross, Teresa of Ávila, and many more. They are saints of the counter-reformation era but not counter-reformation saints. Due to the reforms of a visionary Spanish cardinal long before Father Luther went mad, there was no reformation in Spain that needed countering. This sixteenth-century, Spanish golden age has a counterpart in seventeenth-century France. France in the 1600s produced Saints Francis de Sales, Vincent de Paul, John de Brébeuf, Isaac Jogues, Margaret Mary Alacoque, Jane Frances de Chantal and today's saint, John Eudes, among many other men and women outstanding in holiness. The reforms of the Council of Trent were slow to be implemented in France, but their seeds eventually sprouted abundant spiritual, theological, and missionary fruit, including the founding of Québec, Canada, and Ville Marie de Montreal, a specifically Catholic settlement.

John Eudes was born to pious but uneducated parents in a tiny town in Normandy just as the hot religious wars of the 1500s in France simmered to a boil. He was deeply impressed with his Jesuit teachers at a Catholic high school and began to think about religious life. As he fell under the holy sway of some of the great priests of his era, he decided to emulate their pattern of life. He was ordained a priest for a French version of the Oratory of Saint Philip Neri in 1625.

Father John then became a tireless preacher of parish missions for many years. He preferred to preach in a town for at least six weeks in order to counter the widespread religious ignorance of the faithful. He desired of his hearers nothing less than a total change of life, a complete conversion. He used processions, works of theater, mimes, and whatever else he could think of to draw a congregation. Once in his presence, they learned the creed, the sacraments, an examination of conscience, the laws of morality, and all the fundamentals of the faith. Father Eudes preached Christ in full—a total God who demanded a total human response.

Essential to Father Eudes' spirituality was a profound identity with the emotions and humanity of Jesus. He thought that the mysteries of the Word of God are forever unfolding, that there are always hidden depths of Scripture remaining to be discovered. The meaning of the Word of God, both written and in the flesh, will never be exhausted on earth. This means that Christ's divinity is accessed through his humanity but is never exhausted by his humanity. There is always more God to know and more God to love. This accords with Christian common sense. To assert that a passage of Scripture has been understood in its totality is to limit God's providence and to place one's own mind over God's. That Scripture does not contain error is not the sole proof of its perfection. Scripture is inspired not just for being error free but for what it will communicate, one day, in heaven. God, the Lord and Giver of Life in the Holy Spirit, is the primary author of Scripture, meaning divine truths await discovery, and, more subtly, will *always* await discovery.

AUGUST

As a door of entry into the mystery of Christ and His Blessed Mother, Saint John Eudes tirelessly promoted a liturgical feast in honor of the Sacred Heart of Jesus and what he termed the "Holy" Heart of Mary. Saint John's Sacred Heart devotion was more theological, and less anatomical, than the similar devotion advocated by his contemporary, Saint Margaret Mary Alacoque. Christ's heart, for Saint John, was emblematic of His interiority, His hiddenness. It was a symbol of the heart of all mankind encased in the chest of God. John's devotion to the Sacred Heart led, inevitably, to a very high ideal of the Catholic priest as a man after the heart of Christ, a would-be saint who acts in the person of the one high priest, Jesus Christ. This "French school" of theology and spirituality was fresh thinking in the seventeenth century and put a dagger in the heart of any conception of the priest as a Church bureaucrat who merely performs rituals, for a certain price, to dispense God's grace.

John suffered grievous calumnies and attacks from many in the Church when he left the Oratory to start his own Congregation of secular priests. His promotion of a feast to the Sacred Heart also incurred enemies who misunderstand his theology. The Congregation of Jesus and Mary, commonly known as the Eudists, is still active in parish missions and in teaching in several countries, though France's historic anti-Catholicism removed them from many of their prior apostolates. There is presently an active effort in the Holy See, spearheaded by French priests and bishops, to have Saint John Eudes declared a Doctor of the Church.

Saint John Eudes, your deep identification with the person, emotions, and heart of Jesus Christ inspired all who heard and knew you. May your tireless pastoral efforts, life of prayer, preaching, and writing give powerful example to all priests, whose sacramental dignity you championed.

AUGUST

August 20: Saint Bernard of Clairvaux, Abbot and Doctor
1090–1153
Memorial; Liturgical Color: White
Patron Saint of the Cistercian Order, beekeepers, and candlemakers

A reformer par excellence, he saved the Benedictine Order and rejuvenated monasticism

Today's saint was like a medieval rock star who never stopped touring Europe. He traveled with an entourage, drew enormous crowds, was wildly popular, and called the cream of society his friends. The details of Saint Bernard's life, though he lived before even Saint Francis of Assisi, the Magna Carta, and Dante, are abundantly documented. He was nearly as prolific a writer as Saint Augustine, but primarily via letters, not thick books. And these letters outline his character in sharp profile. He was intelligent, emotion laden, erudite, forceful, and contemplative. He spoke and wrote poetically, beautifully, clearly, and deeply. Pope Pius XII called him "the last of the Fathers" of the Church.

Bernard was born in a castle to a highborn family and was sent away by his parents during his youth to receive a classical education. After the death of his mother left him in a depression, he pondered more seriously what God wanted of him. When Bernard was a child, in his native region of Southeastern France, a local monk decided to try something new. He founded a new monastery at a place called Cîteaux in the hope of living the Benedictine Rule with exactitude and rigor. At the age of twenty-two, still mourning his mother, Bernard decided to dedicate his life to God and to enter this new, experimental monastery. But Bernard being Bernard, with all the force of his mind and personality, when he knocked on the door of the abbey, he was not alone. Behind him at the door stood a long train of thirty of his brothers, cousins, and friends, all noblemen. Bernard was the leader. They were the followers. They wanted to become monks because he wanted to become a monk. When he asked, they answered, and they answered "Yes." This natural gift to command and lead was a sign of things to come.

Cîteaux inspired and gave its name to the Cistercian movement of monastic reform. Because of Bernard's dynamic presence, Cîteaux soon overflowed with monks, and Bernard was sent, as Abbot, to found a new monastery at Clairvaux, or Clear Valley. This was his base for the rest of his itinerant life. As the first Abbot of Clairvaux, Bernard stamped the Cistercian movement with its distinctive character: sobriety in art and architecture, solemnity in liturgy, austerity in life, industriousness in labor, strictness in observance of the Rule, and silence pervading all. Cîteaux gave birth to Clairvaux, and Clairvaux spawned a vast Cistercian family that considers Bernard its founder. By the time of Bernard's death, there were 343 Cistercian monasteries the length and breadth of Europe.

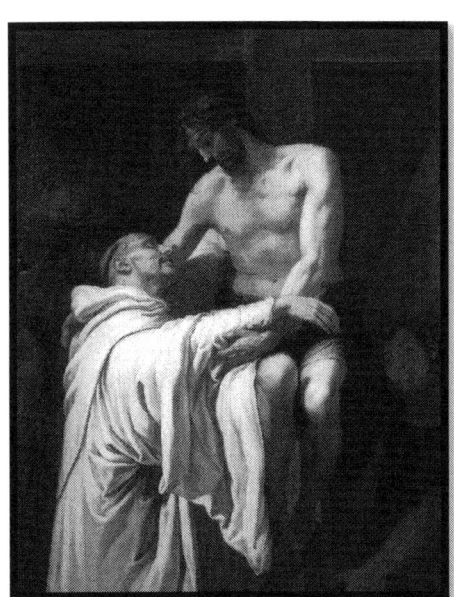

Christ Embracing St. Bernard
Francisco Ribalta

For an austere contemplative monk, Bernard, ironically, spent much of his life on the road. His gifts were such that he was consulted by princes, kings, and popes on every imaginable issue. He participated in Church councils, mediated civil conflicts, inaugurated Crusades, and wrote long commentaries on prayer, theology, and Scripture. He had to employ secretaries, like a minister of state, who recorded the prodigious correspondence that flowed constantly from his mouth. He became famous as a miraculous healer. Crowds of people lined his route to receive his blessing or to feel his hands press against their skulls. In one incident, after wading into a large, clamoring crowd desiring his miraculous touch, he had to fight to return to his lodging as the people tore at his habit. A wit wrote that the real miracle was not his healing, but that Bernard escaped alive.

Bernard's authentic and tender devotion to the Virgin Mary was expressed sublimely in his writings. For his Marian devotion, eloquence, and contemplative spirit, Bernard substitutes for Beatrice as Dante takes the final steps of his mythical voyage toward God in the Divine Comedy. In the blazing fire of pure love that is the Beatific Vision, Bernard is at Dante's side as their eyes drink in the vision of a splendid, holographic, white rose emanating like a vision from the Godhead's bright light. The Queen of this mystical white rose is the Virgin, and "faithful Bernard" gazes in silent admiration at the woman he loves so dearly. Saint Bernard was canonized in 1174 and named a Doctor of the Church in 1830.

Saint Bernard, may we see in your devotion to Mary, endless travels, strict life, and keen eye for beauty, the model of an educated and devoted monk. Intercede for all religious, and for all those with a contemplative heart who are in the world, to love God half as well as you did.

August 21: Saint Pius X, Pope
1835–1914
Memorial; Liturgical Color: White
Patron Saint of First Communicants and pilgrims

Born humble and poor, he never forgot his origins while in the Chair of St. Peter

In the long span of three hundred and forty years between the death of Pope Saint Pius V in 1572 and today's pope-saint, who died in 1914, not one pope is a canonized saint. It is a sign of the Church's solid foundations and rock-like durability that less than holy men have normally led her, and still she has thrived. Analogous to the doctrine of *ex opere operato*, which holds that a sacrament's grace is communicated by merely being performed, the headship of the universal Church is exercised well by intelligent men who care for her good, even if they are not personally holy. But that a pope be holy makes the Church even more impressive, in the same way that a priest's holiness doesn't make a sacrament more a sacrament but does make it more fruitful.

Pope Saint Pius X was born Giuseppe Sarto in Northern Italy to humble parents in a poor home, the second of ten children. He entered the seminary as an adolescent and was ordained a priest at the young age of twenty-three. He served for many years in parishes and seminaries before being made a bishop and then a cardinal. His life experience in the Church was almost exclusively pastoral, that is, concerned with the care of souls. He was not a university professor, Vatican diplomat, scholar, or ecclesiastical bureaucrat. He was the only pope of the twentieth century without a doctoral degree. He was a parish priest, confessor, spiritual director, and boots-on-the-ground diocesan bishop. His rural background and forthright view of the faith lent Pius a common touch which sympathized with the faith of the "everyman" who fill the pews on Sunday morning. But Pius' past limited him somewhat as well. In his desire to protect the faithful from error like a good father protects his children, he could be overly suspicious of, and reactionary toward, a great deal of theological scholarship that would later be absorbed into the universal body of Christ at the Second Vatican Council.

Pius X made changes to the Church's liturgical and sacramental life that proved to be enduring and popular. He lowered the age of First Holy Communion from twelve to seven and encouraged frequent reception of Holy Communion instead of the once-a-year, Easter Duty reception that was then typical. Pius simplified the Breviary, the book of Psalms that priests and nuns pray every day, encouraged the use of Gregorian chant at Mass, and mandated that the Confraternity of Christian Doctrine (CCD) be present in every parish in the world to teach catechism to children. He also began the enormous process of gathering and synthesizing the Church's massive, centuries' old body of law into an easy to handle Code of Canon Law which was promulgated in 1917.

Pius reacted strongly and negatively toward various schools of theological scholarship he lumped under the imprecise title of "Modernism." Pius was intransigent and relentless in weeding out from the garden of the Church all those with non-scholastic methods and conclusions in philosophy and theology. That is, he distrusted research and teaching not rooted in the approach of Saint Thomas Aquinas and similar medieval thinkers. The "Modernist" approach to ancient texts, language studies, scriptural analysis, church history, comparative theology, etc. would eventually become standard in Catholicism. But it took many decades for these more critical approaches to merge with theological orthodoxy, deep spirituality, and fidelity to Rome in the powerful synthesis taught by Vatican II and beyond.

Saint Pius X stayed humble and poor his entire life. He was embarrassed by the pomp of papal ceremonies but nonetheless understood their significance to the faithful. Three of his unmarried sisters lived in near poverty on the outskirts of Rome while he reigned as pope. He could have, but did not, favor them with titles or other privileges to ease their burdens. Pius died the same month as the guns of August roared a start to World War I. His death resulted partly from a deep melancholy that Christian Europe had once again devolved into such conflict. He was canonized in 1954.

Pope Saint Pius X, your doctrinal fidelity, Eucharistic piety, and devotion to Mary were exemplary. May your simplicity of life, common touch, and bravery in fighting the enemies of the Church, inspire all who lead the Body of Christ on earth in whatever capacity.

August 22: Queenship of the Blessed Virgin Mary

Memorial; Liturgical Color: White

The mother of a king is a queen who receives honor in her son's realm

Mary is both a queen and a mother, but she is more mother than queen. Mary's Queenship and "mothership," or motherhood, spark to life simultaneously. In the very moment Mary becomes a mother at the Annunciation, she also becomes a queen. The Archangel Gabriel tells Mary that her Son will sit on "the throne of his ancestor David" and that "He will reign over the house of Jacob forever, and of his kingdom there will be no end" (Lk 1:32–33). Since Jesus is a king, and since He is conceived in the womb of Mary, and since in Israel the mother of a king was always a queen, (the daughter not necessarily so), Mary becomes a queen. Some texts from the early centuries of the Church call Mary the "domina," the female of "dominus," Latin for "master" or "Lord."

It is not royal blood, but her motherly relationship, that makes Mary a queen. And since nothing is excluded from the realm of Christ the

AUGUST

King, Mary is the Queen of that same realm, including both heaven and earth. This realm was not earned through violent conquest or political machinations. The Kingdom of Christ the King was purchased through a blood sacrifice of the King Himself who died on the cross. Soldiers were not killed so that Christ could walk over their corpses on the battlefield in order to rule a vanquished people from a secular throne. No, of course not. Christ humbly allowed Himself to be murdered so that He could rise forty hours later and ascend into heaven to be seated, like a king, at the right hand of the Father. (Kings sit. Their audience's stand.) Christ gives the world a new form of reigning, a reinterpretation of the words "I win!"

Mary is that heavenly queen in the mysterious vision of the Book of Revelation in which appears "a woman clothed with the sun, with the moon under her feet, and on her head a crown of twelve stars" (Rv 12:1–3). The complex symbolism of this crowned empress encompasses Mary, Israel, and the Church Herself. Mary's coronation, the Fifth Glorious Mystery of the rosary, has not been defined dogmatically but has been celebrated liturgically and depicted in art since early medieval times.

The most ancient depiction of Mary as queen is a mosaic from the 500s in a small church in the historic center of Rome! But the feast day of her Queenship was only placed in the Church's calendar in 1954. Vatican II stated unequivocally that "Mary was taken up body and soul into heavenly glory, and exalted by the Lord as Queen of the universe..." *(Lumen Gentium*, 59). After the liturgical reforms of Vatican II, the octave of Mary's Assumption was abrogated but is still recalled in her Queenship being commemorated eight days after August 15, showing the link between the two celebrations.

Earthly kings, queens, and kingdoms, so present throughout the lived history of mankind, are, more cosmically, images or signs of the structure of authority that lies behind all creation. Mankind naturally organizes its public life to ensure peaceful co-existence with others, to promote order and tranquility, and to foster the common good in a thousand ways. This secular response of establishing a structure to manage together what cannot be managed alone is universal and always includes certain leaders to represent the organized community. All of this has a religious equivalent. A sacred canopy hangs over the world. A timeless, divine megastructure encompasses under itself all of the smaller, temporary civic structures. The man anointed as king, the woman crowned as queen, the order they impose through a just rule in a secular polity, point to something else—an underlying, and overarching, sacred polity in which God rules His creation like a fatherly king. In this timeless theological union, the feminine presence is felt. The queen mother is there, interceding with her King-Son on behalf of His subjects. She worships with them but also receives their honor. The accolades directed at her are deflected, mirror-like, to the greater One to whom she is holy daughter, holy mother, holy spouse and holy queen, our life, our sweetness, and our hope.

Mary, Queen of the Universe, in your Son's Kingdom, the faithful struggle to be faithful and to be fruitful. We are under your regal yet maternal care. May we please both our King and Father, and you, our Queen and Mother, since all parents are deserving of their children's honor.

August 23: Saint Rose of Lima, Virgin
1586–1617
Optional Memorial; Liturgical Color: White
Patron Saint of Peru, florists, and gardeners

America's first saint, she conquered herself by direct attack

Today's saint was born Isabel Flores de Oliva in colonial Spain, today's Peru, to a middle-class Catholic family. She took the name "Rose" when she was confirmed by Lima's bishop, the future Saint Turibius of Mogrovejo. "Rose" had been her nickname since infancy after a servant said that she was as beautiful as a rose. Young Rose was indeed beautiful and attracted the attention of various suitors. But she had decided from a young age to give herself to Christ alone, so she actively deterred male interest by cutting off her hair, rubbing pepper into her pure skin to blister her face, and by damaging her feminine hands with the acidic juice of limes.

Her natural affinity for the things of God was not reciprocated by her father, who blocked her desire to enter a Dominican convent as a nun. Instead, Rose became a Third Order Dominican, a lay woman dedicated to living Catholicism in accord with Dominican spiritual ideals outside of the cloister. But Rose pushed her Third Order spirituality beyond its natural limits. She lived poverty, chastity, obedience and numerous other virtues far more rigorously than most professed nuns. Bending somewhat to his daughter's desires, Rose's father allowed her to live apart from the family in a small hut on his property. From that hut, and from a room in the family home where she cared for the sick and the poor, Rose became famous throughout Lima.

St. Rose of Lima

Rose's fame was due to her generous care for the sick and, perhaps most of all, due to her extraordinary austerities and some related miraculous events. Rose's spiritual model was Saint Catherine of Siena, the fourteenth-century Italian mystic who was also a Dominican tertiary. Saint Catherine also lived at home, was from a large family like Rose, and had a high, a very high, threshold for physical pain and suffering, just like Rose. Rose did not fast merely on certain days or at certain times. She fasted from life itself. She seemingly ate only Holy Communion. What little she did consume she would often force herself to vomit up afterward. She ate no meat, slept on a bed of tile shards, and wore a crown, disguised with flowers, equipped with small spikes which pierced the thin, taut skin wrapped over her skull.

Saint Rose's short life was, on one hand, the full, ripened fruit of sixteenth-century Spanish mysticism—pious, mortifying, Christocentric, and theologically orthodox. From a different perspective, Rose's sustained and extreme mortifications were on the far margins of psychologically healthy. Her self-attacks would today be considered expressions of bulimia, mental instability, and self-hating to the point of illness. But Rose is not here to be interviewed on the Freudian couch, and to describe her personality, in any case, is not to judge it. Saint Rose lived a model life for her era, was clearly motivated by love of God, and expressed such control over her natural, corporeal needs that sanctifying grace as her hidden strength cannot be discounted.

Rose died in the perfume of holiness at the age of thirty-one. Her funeral was held in Lima's Cathedral with all local dignitaries in attendance. She was beatified in 1667 and canonized in 1671. She is interred in the same church as Saint Martin de Porres in central Lima. Her pre-Vatican II feast day of August 30 is a national holiday in Peru, and her image graces that country's highest denomination currency. She is known as a powerful miracle worker credited with numerous physical healings unto today.

Saint Rose of Lima, you were young and holy. You dedicated your body and soul to God while still a child. Through your example and through your heavenly intercession, help all Catholics, especially the young, to dedicate their lives to God from the very start.

August 24: Saint Bartholomew, Apostle
First Century
Feast; Liturgical Color: Red
Patron Saint of bookbinders, butchers, and leather workers

The Church conquered an imperfect world due to the heroic witness of the Apostles

Little is known with certainty about today's Apostle, and perhaps Saint Bartholomew is just fine with that. If he were like Saint John the Baptist, he would want Christ to increase and himself to decrease. It is possible, although not certain, that Bartholomew is the same Apostle as Nathaniel. Bartholomew means "Son of Tolmai" and is not a name, technically, but a patronymic, like the Scandinavian "son" found in "Anderson" or "Erikson." The Bartholomew of Matthew, Mark, and Luke may describe the man known in the Gospel of John more correctly as Nathaniel. Bartholomew is paired with Philip in some Gospel lists, which corresponds, interestingly, with Philip being an old friend of Nathaniel in John's Gospel. But so little is known with certainty about the Apostles that these conjectures will likely never be resolved.

AUGUST

After his appearance in the Gospels, Bartholomew first resurfaces almost three hundred years later in the works of Eusebius, a bishop and church historian who wrote around 300 A.D. Eusebius relates a story about a Christian teacher traveling in India who is told that an Apostle, presumably Bartholomew, had preached there long before him and had brought a Hebrew Gospel with him. Equally vague traditions have Bartholomew evangelizing in Persia, Armenia, Mesopotamia, and Egypt. The details of his death likewise dissipated in the fog of ancient history. One tradition holds that he was flayed alive, a story reflected in Michelangelo's *Last Judgment* in the Sistine Chapel, which depicts Bartholomew holding his own skin. Because of this tradition, Bartholomew is the patron saint of tanners. History holds that Bartholomew's relics are in the church named after him on an island in Rome's Tiber River.

The Nicene Creed states that we believe in One, Holy, Catholic, and Apostolic Church. The Church, then, is an object of faith in the same way that God is an object of faith. She is not the end result of a world-wide community of believers or merely a forum for belief. She gathers. She is not gathered. The Church is the mother of Christians, not their offspring. The Church is more than a carrier of faith, more than a train whose cargo barrels through the centuries transporting the heavy freight of the Gospels and tradition to diverse cultures. The Church not only bears a message, then, She is the message.

Unfortunately, the Church's sins and failings are, for many, the primary obstacle to belief in Christ. It is not just that the Church's holiness is not apparent. It is that Her unity is questioned due to deep theological divisions. And Her members' struggles for power, wealth, and prestige also obscure a more pristine Christian faith which She should project. But to think that the Church could be sublimely holy, totally unified, and pristinely sinless is to dream. The Church exists in the world, reflects the world's dramas, and suffers from Her same sins. We do not believe in the Church because She is perfect, but because there is nothing else like Her. She is unique. She is better than any alternative. If we expect from the Church the Sacraments, we will never be disappointed.

Today's saint lived and evangelized in the era of the dreamy early church, when the fire of Christ's love burned hottest, when the

Gospel was as fresh as baked bread, and when gusts of the Holy Spirit blew through the Apostles' hair. And yet...Bartholomew still had his skin slowly peeled from his body by a sharp knife, or was crucified, or both. The world was wicked in the first century too, and so the Church had problems in that era as well. Just read the letters of Saint Paul. The Church was born into a rough pagan world and still exists in a rough, though different, secular world. Saint Bartholomew died at the hands of imperfect pagans for an imperfect Church. Yet the imperfect, primitive Church persevered in her infancy because of the witness and sacrifice of many saints. The imperfect, modern Church will continue to persevere in Her adulthood because of our witness and sacrifice today.

Saint Bartholomew, help all Christians to see in your example of martyrdom a heroic witness to perseverance in the face of difficulty, of fidelity in the face of doubt, and of courage in the face of timidity. May we have just a portion of what you had in such abundance.

August 25: Saint Louis
1214–1270
Optional Memorial; Liturgical Color: White
Patron Saint of barbers, grooms, and Saint Louis, Missouri

A king leads in piety, mortification, and faith, and dies crusading for the King of all

Jesus said, "If any want to become my followers, let them deny themselves and take up their cross and follow me" (Mt 16:24). Today's saint fulfilled Christ's commandment in two ways. First and most obviously, King Louis IX of France, or Saint Louis, took up his cross by practicing serious physical mortifications his entire life. He wore a hair shirt, fasted, never took God's name in vain, and would not tell jokes or even laugh on Fridays. Secondly, he had a cloth cross woven onto his tunic and thus became a knight crusader. Louis and countless other medieval knights understood the commandment to "take up their cross" to be fulfilled not merely through physical mortification but by wading into battle with the sign of Christ on their chests. That visible cloth cross boldly proclaimed a man's commitment to liberating the Holy Land from Muslim control through hard battle.

AUGUST

When Louis was a child his mother told him, "I would rather see you dead at my feet than that you should ever commit a mortal sin." He never forgot her words. After his father's early death, Louis was crowned, or anointed, king in the quasi-liturgical ceremony whose main elements can still be seen at modern coronations. He married at twenty, and he and his wife had eleven children. He was totally devoted to Christ and the Church. He prayed the breviary every day, attended daily Mass, and constructed stunning churches, including Paris' Saint Chapelle to house his collection of relics, including the true Cross of Christ. He was so disturbed by the sin of blasphemy that he promulgated a law that all blasphemers be branded on the lips. He waged war against the Cathars of Southern France and, together with the Dominicans and the Inquisition, vanquished their heretical movement.

Louis possessed an elusive charisma that made people not only want to be in his presence but also to touch his person. He was well educated, friendly, curious, and truly humble. Every man was his friend. He invited the quiet Saint Thomas Aquinas, who was studying in Paris at the time, over to dinner for the joy of theological conversation. He promulgated laws respecting the presumption of innocence and due process for everyone. He was, in short, a model Christian king who reigned over a golden century in which France was the largest, most unified, and wealthiest kingdom in Europe.

Despite his fame and the creature comforts of home, Louis made the courageous, if reckless, decision to personally lead two crusades. The first was initially successful but ended disastrously with Louis's capture and his army being crushed in battle. Only a king's ransom secured his release. The second crusade he embarked on was even more disastrous. King Louis died of typhus, along with many men in his camp, on the shores of modern Tunisia, having just begun their journey. One of his last acts was to kneel by his bed to receive Holy Communion. He had wanted to die a martyr, or a confessor, for the faith. His desire was not technically fulfilled. But he did give his life sacrificially in the noble, centuries-long, quixotic quest to reconquer Jerusalem and the Holy Land for Christian pilgrimage. He was canonized in 1297.

AUGUST

ST. LOUIS
August 25

"I advise you that you accustom yourself to frequent confession, and that you choose always, as your confessors, men who are upright and sufficiently learned, and who can teach you what you should do and what you should avoid."

– From a letter of St. Louis to his son Philip III

AUGUST

Saint Louis of France, you were intrepid in your love for Christ and the Church. Impart from heaven to all modern Catholics some of your same daring spirit—to be courageous in living and spreading the faith, to give and not count the cost.

August 25: Saint Joseph Calasanz, Priest
1556–1648
Optional Memorial; Liturgical Color: White
<u>Patron Saint of Catholic schools and school children</u>

A visionary implements his plan, is defamed, and forgives

The star of today's saint burns less brightly than others in the great constellation of counter-reformation saints. But the educational vision of Saint Joseph Calasanz and the ultimate spread and triumph of his order after his death have had an enduring impact far exceeding his humble reputation.

Calasanz was born into a minor noble family in Spain, the youngest of eight children. His parents valued education and sent their boy to religious schools to receive a fine training in the classics. While a teenager, he decided that God was calling him to be a priest. After finishing his university studies with distinction, he was ordained in 1583. He carried out several sensitive and important pastoral and administrative duties for his local bishop and then made a life-altering decision. In 1592 he resigned his appointments, gave away his inheritance to his sisters, funded some worthy projects for the needy, and departed for Rome. He would live there for the next fifty-six years of his long life.

Like his Roman contemporary Saint Philip Neri, Joseph saw the pressing need to educate the great mass of poor children who spent their days doing everything except going to school. With the assistance of highly placed connections in the Church and Roman nobility, Joseph was given rent-free space in a parish where he offered free classes to poor children. The only schools in existence at the time were tuition based. Without knowing it, Joseph had done something revolutionary. He had started the first free school in modern Europe, although similar initiatives were quick to follow. Joseph's free school for the poor immediately exploded in size to over a thousand students. He and his co-workers quickly founded similar schools in other regions of Italy, became more disciplined in their approach, and sought, and received, official status in the Church. In 1622 the pope approved the Order of Poor Clerks Regular of the Mother of God of the Pious Schools, or the Piarists, as they were commonly known. They were the first order of priests dedicated to primary school education.

While his successful educational vision was being implemented, Joseph's work provoked envy among the upper classes, clerics included, who resented educating, for free, the lower echelon of society. Joseph also aroused suspicion for his personal friendship with Galileo Galilei, who was under investigation by Church authorities for his theory that the earth moved around the sun. Crises internal to the Piarists concerning the sin that dare not speak its name caused even greater alarm. All of these pressures and intrigues led to Joseph's arrest and humiliation by the Inquisition for a brief period in 1642. Two of his own Piarist priests were his most bitter enemies, and, in their attempts to cover up their own sins and incompetence, they pulled every lever of influence they could put their hands on to remove Joseph as the head of his own order. Joseph was not bitter, said it was the Lord's will, and forgave them. Due to its internal problems, however, the order was suppressed in 1646.

When Joseph died in 1648 at the age of ninety, his life-work had been obliterated. But the Piarists were resurrected in the following decades, thrived, and opened schools in various countries. Piarist fathers helped stem the Protestant tide in Poland, educated luminaries such as Mozart, Haydn, Schubert, and Goya, and provided the model for free public schools later adopted by Saint Jean-Baptiste de La Salle and Saint John Bosco. Joseph Calasanz was canonized in 1767 "a perpetual miracle of fortitude and another Job" in the words of a pope.

Saint Joseph Calasanz, you were disgraced, defamed, maligned and imprisoned and yet forgave all who had robbed you of your most precious personal possession: your reputation. Help us to be so forgiving toward those who steal from us what we have taken so long to build up.

AUGUST

August 27: Saint Monica
c. 331–387
Memorial; Liturgical Color: White
Patron Saint of difficult marriages, homemakers, and mothers

Without her example of persevering prayer, her gifted son would not have converted

Most of the female saints of the first few centuries of the Church are virgins, martyrs, or both. Most of the medieval and modern female saints are nuns, especially foundresses of religious orders. Married female saints are relatively rare. With some few contemporary exceptions, they are the mothers of kings, of emperors, or of other canonized saints. Saint Monica is the mother of Saint Augustine. She was raised in a Catholic family in long extinct Christian North Africa, probably in the small town of Tagaste in modern day Algeria. Tagaste had been Christian for over two hundred and fifty years by the time Monica was born. So although from a present-day perspective she was born in ancient times, just after the Council of Nicea, her family's faith likely dated to the first waves of African Christianity, long before Nicea.

Monica had at least three children: Navigius, Perpetua, and her oldest and dearest son, Augustine. No mother can be reduced just to what they mean to their children, yet it is due exclusively to her son Augustine that so much is known about the life of Monica. Augustine seemed to never stop writing, and after God and Augustine himself, Monica is the central character in his autobiography, the *Confessions*. Monica is ever concerned about, and ever present to, Augustine. She won't let him out of her sight.

When Augustine is preparing to sail for Italy from the port at Carthage, he is surprised to learn that his mother intends to travel with him. So he deceives her about the ship's departure time and escapes without her. But she is persistent. She later follows him to Rome only to find that he has moved on. So she follows him to Milan, finds him, and moves in with him and his friends. It is no wonder that Augustine wrote: "She liked to have me with her, as mothers do, but far more than most mothers."

AUGUST

Monica married a man named Patricius and converted him, at least superficially. He was a difficult man whose early death left her a widow at forty. Monica and her husband wanted their gifted son Augustine to receive the best education possible, so they sent him away for schooling. And there Augustine fell into the serious and enduring moral and theological errors which would form the central drama of Monica's life. It is said that all of the plots in the world can be reduced to just five or six. One of those is "Get back home." Saint Monica's life was dedicated to getting her son back to his home, the Church. She wept, she prayed, she fasted. Nothing seemed to work for fifteen years while her son strayed far from the Catholic path, seemingly without remorse.

In the midst of her spiritual trials and sufferings over Augustine, Monica had a vision. She was standing on a wooden beam. A bright, fluorescent being told her to dry her eyes, for "your son is with you." Monica told Augustine about the vision. He responded that yes, they could indeed be together if she would just abandon her faith. Monica immediately retorted: "He didn't say that I was with you. He said that you were with me." Augustine never forgot her quick and insightful answer.

In Milan, Monica befriended the great Saint Ambrose, who played such a key role in Augustine's conversion. The seed of her prayers bore fruit when Augustine abandoned his sinful life, was baptized, and decided to return to North Africa as a Christian leader. Her son had come home to the Church and was returning to his native land. Her life's mission accomplished, Saint Monica died in her late fifties in the Roman port of Ostia, while waiting to board the ship to cross over to Africa. In her final hours, Augustine asked if he should transport her body to Tagaste for burial next to her husband. She said she was happy to be buried wherever she died, for "nothing is far from God." Her remains are now found in the Basilica of Saint Augustine in central Rome.

Saint Monica, you were persevering in your efforts to straighten the crooked paths of your son's life. Your prayers, pilgrimages, fasts, and words were fruitful, but only after many tears. Help us to be as concerned as you for the immortal souls of those who are close to us.

August 28: Saint Augustine, Bishop and Doctor
354–430
Memorial; Liturgical Color: White
<u>*Patron Saint of theologians and printers*</u>

A psychologist, theologian, and working bishop is the greatest convert after Saint Paul

The mighty African Saint Augustine climbed the heights of thought, stood upright on their peaks, and turned toward Rome, and thus spread his long, deep shadow over the entire globe. As a Christian thinker, he has few equals. He is *the* saint of the first millennium. Augustine was born in the small Roman village of Tagaste, in Northern Africa, to a minor civil official and a pious, head-strong mother. Tagaste had no swagger. Its simple people were bent over from working the land since time immemorial. The great African cities hugged the Mediterranean coast, far from Tagaste, which was cut off, two hundred miles inland. When he was a boy, Augustine imagined what the far-off waves of the sea were like by peering into a glass of water. When he was twenty-eight, he descended from his native hills and sailed for Rome to find himself, God, and holy fame. When he returned to Africa many years later, it was for good. The hot-tempered young African had matured into a cool-headed spiritual father. He was now their bishop, lovingly and tirelessly serving the open, forthright townsmen that were his natural kin.

It is challenging to categorize someone who is the founder of an entire genre or school of thought. No one knew what an autobiography was until Augustine wrote his *Confessions*. There was Caesar's *Gallic War* before, and there would be Jean-Jacques Rousseau's *Confessions* later. And there is volume after volume now. All pale. Augustine wrote the *Confessions* as the Bishop of Hippo when he was about forty-three, covering his early life up to the age of thirty-three. It is not a great book due to its density of historical detail. The reader hungers for facts and is left unsatisfied. Whereas autobiographies are normally stuffed with people, places, and things, Augustine says almost nothing about his father, only mentioning his death in passing. He does not clarify how many siblings he has. It is often not clear when, or where, events occur. Augustine is clearly not concerned, in short, with his outward

AUGUST

journey. It is the inner drama, the drama of the soul, that he wants to recount. The *Confessions* changes the answer to the perennial question "What really happened?" from the outside to the inside. Augustine is the author of the first "Story of a Soul."

Augustine is the world's first great psychologist. He does self-reflection and analyses ages before Saint Ignatius and perceives unconscious motivations centuries before Freud. The painfully self-aware, tell-you-everything, what-are-you-hiding, hyper-modern psyche of today is deformed Augustinianism. It took a long time for the future to catch up to him. Augustine does so many things first, does them better, and does them as a Catholic. With the historical details left to the side, he self-investigates his early childhood, his unsatisfied father-hunger, the emotional darkness caused by the death of friends, his enduring guilt for stealing some pears, his complex love for his mother, and how hard it is…how hard…to leave the woman he has loved for fifteen years. They have a child together after all. But Augustine must let her go. He must move on, and he does. She is the *Confessions'* mysterious character. He never even gives her name.

Reading other great theologians, one knows almost nothing about them, their friends, or their personal thoughts or desires. Reading Augustine, you get the man in full. He is concerned with relationships, that of his to God and to his mother, and that of others to himself. He would start his personal letters with *Dulcissimus concivis—My dearest friend*. And he meant it. He was a highly educated scholar, a great letter writer who worked in the close orbit of the Roman imperial court, and a sophisticated thinker who most opened the intellectual path the Church would walk until the scholastics of medieval times introduced Aristotle to Christian thought.

When Augustine turned his head from the beauty of the senses toward the holy beauty of God, his personal sensory privation was more than an absence. It was a total commitment. In the second phase of his life, Augustine placed the heavy cross of routine pastoral care on his shoulders. He became a working bishop and excelled at this role. This complex man, this highly fruitful, working intellectual, asked to be alone in his room when death finally came for him in his seventy-fifth year.

AUGUST

Saint Augustine, may our own examination of conscience be like yours—continual, honest, and Christ-centered. You achieved a high level of self-awareness not for its own sake but to prune all sin from your soul. May we be as self-focused, and as God-focused, as you were.

August 29: The Passion of Saint John the Baptist, Martyr
c. 29 A.D.
<u>Memorial; Liturgical Color: Red</u>

A desert-dwelling, locust-eating, weed-wearing, celibate ascetic dies for marriage

Saint John Vianney was so opposed to the dances held routinely in his small town of Ars that he dedicated a small chapel in his parish church to Saint John the Baptist. At its entrance was painted, perhaps somewhat tongue in cheek, a warning of the evil effects produced by lust and drink: "His head was the price of a dance." Saint John the Baptist's head was, indeed, the wage rendered by an older man for the satisfaction of watching a young girl dance at his birthday party. More remotely, however, John's beheading was not caused by a suggestive dance. He paid with his head for poking the bear. John denounced King Herod Antipas, to his face, for divorcing his lawful wife and taking as his own Herodias, his sister-in-law, the wife of his still living half-brother Philip. (Convoluted family blood lines also made Herodias Herod's niece.) John the Baptist died a martyr for marriage.

Herod Antipas was a tetrarch—one of four rulers who co-governed ancient Palestine as client kings under the oversight of a Roman governor. Herod Antipas learned cruelty at home on his father's knee. His father, Herod the Great, had two of his own sons strangled to death, murdered his favorite wife, and ordered the slaughter of all the male babies of Bethlehem. Herod Antipas' imprisonment and execution of John was more aggressive than his restrained interaction, a few years later, with John's cousin. Jesus had called Herod a "fox" when some pharisees told Jesus that Herod was plotting His death. Pontius Pilate later sent Jesus to Herod for interrogation after Pilate determined that the Jew's complaints about Jesus fell more under Herod's jurisdiction than Pilate's own. At this strange audience in Jerusalem between Herod and Jesus on Good Friday, Herod wanted Jesus to perform a miracle for him, as if Jesus were a mere magician who pulled rabbits out of hats. But Jesus said not a word to the man who killed His beloved cousin. Jesus, after all, did not come to provide bread and circuses to the curious. He performed miracles to elicit and to reward faith. So the fox sent Jesus back to Pilate for what always happened next.

Herod is to John the Baptist what Pilate is to Jesus. Neither Herod's nor Pilate's first choice was to order an execution. But cowardice and fear coalesced until commanding the death of an innocent man was more expedient than braving the ridicule and threats of subordinates. According to Saint Mark, "Herod feared John,

The beheading of St. John the Baptist
Michelangelo Merisi da Caravaggio

knowing that he was a righteous and holy man...When he heard him, he was greatly perplexed; and yet he liked to listen to him" (Mk 6: 20). "[Herod] was deeply grieved" (Mk 6: 26) that he had to order John's death. But he didn't actually have to order John's death. If he were truly grieved, he could have stood up in the midst of the happy crowd, said "I made a stupid promise which I now regret," and granted Salome (her name is not found in the Bible) some other handsome gift instead of a blood-splattered plate. Herod beheaded a man to save face, to avoid embarrassment, and to avoid having to say "I made a mistake."

AUGUST

The Passion, or Beheading, of Saint John the Baptist is one of the very oldest liturgical feasts on the Church's calendar. John's birth may be *the* oldest feast. Along with the feasts of Holy Week, the original event of John's death is right there on the surface of Holy Scripture, and so likely was commemorated as soon as the Church started commemorating anything. John the Baptist's colorful life on the edge of respectability came to an abrupt end due to the weakness of a weak man, Herod, and due to the revenge sought by the troubled conscience of Herodias, who despised John for mentioning the obvious. Saint Jerome writes that Herodias's rage was not satiated by the grisly head of her tormentor on a platter, but that she rabidly stabbed the tongue which had indicted her even after it was silenced.

Saint John the Baptist, your penitential life ended abruptly when you spoke the truth to power. You did not flinch, vacillate, or equivocate. You were imprisoned and then killed for defending the dignity of marriage. Help us to be as courageous and plain-spoken as you.

SEPTEMBER

The Exaltation of the Holy Cross

The Crucifixion – Léon Bonnat

SEPTEMBER

September 3: Saint Gregory the Great, Pope and Doctor
c. 540–604
Memorial; Liturgical Color: White
Patron Saint of musicians, singers, students, and teachers

A gifted nobleman serves Rome, becomes a monk, and then a consequential pope

When your salad is *awesome*, your car *amazing*, and your internet connection is *great*, there's a problem. Overused superlatives diminish their own meaning and crowd the linguistic space reserved for things which are truly *awesome*, *amazing*, and *great*. Today's saint sent the large missionary party that trekked across Europe and converted Saxon England to Catholicism, establishing a culture that endured for almost a millennium. That's *awesome*! He wrote a theological work that was used for centuries by thousands of bishops to help them become more fatherly pastors. That's *amazing*! Gregorian chant is named after him; he is one of the four Latin Fathers of the Church; he was the first pope to use "Servant of the Servants of God" as a papal title; he alone preserved the memory of Saint Benedict with a biography; he made revisions to the content and structure of the Mass which are part of the liturgy until today; and he was the most impactful pope of the long span of centuries from the 500s to the 1000s. That's *great*! These accomplishments thus truly merit the title Great with which Saint Gregory has been justly crowned by history.

Pope Saint Gregory the Great was born into a noble Roman family with a history of service to Church and empire. The family home was perched on one of Rome's seven ancient hills, the Caelian, which Via San Gregorio still cuts through today. His father was a Roman senator, although at a time when Italy was in decline and the imperial government was based in Constantinople. Gregory received an education in keeping with his class and became the Prefect of Rome, its highest civil position, in his early thirties. In 579 he was chosen by the pope as his emissary to the emperor's court in Constantinople, primarily to seek the emperor's assistance in protecting Italy from the Lombard tribes that had long ago overrun her.

Gregory was elected the bishop of his home city in 590 and was thus obligated to abandon the quiet life of a monk, which he had been living with some friends for a few years in a small monastery near his family home. In numerous letters which have fortunately been preserved, Pope Gregory, soon after his election, bemoans the loss of his monastic solitude, peaceful recollection, and life of prayer. But he had only been a monk for a few short years. Gregory's skills as an administrator, honed in his long years of prior civil and church leadership, proved valuable when he sat on the Chair of Saint Peter.

He drew into the orbit of papal authority the bishops of France and Spain who had, until then, been operating somewhat autonomously. He secured the allegiance of Italy's northern tribes to orthodox Catholicism, compelling them to abandon the counterfeit Arian Christianity they had held for centuries. And Gregory made the fateful decision to personally organize and promote the great, and highly successful, missionary journey of Saint Augustine of Canterbury to the Kingdom of Kent in England.

Pope Saint Gregory the Great's legacy in liturgy, pastoral doctrine, and miracles left a deep mark on medieval Europe and beyond. The Council of Trent in 1562 mandated the suppression of votive Mass cycles for the dead or for any other need. But the Council Fathers made one exception: The Mass of Saint Gregory, a cycle of thirty Masses on thirty consecutive days for the release of a soul from purgatory, was not suppressed. Almost a thousand years after his death, Gregory's memory was too venerable to suppress. Gregory was an encourager of the encouragers, a bishop who modeled, strengthened, and explained how and why his fellow bishops should be fathers first and lords second.

Pope Saint Gregory the Great, your example of holy leadership, of scholarly practicality, of balance between universal and local concerns, helps all Christians to weigh their many duties in a proper balance and to choose correctly what matters most to God and their own salvation.

SEPTEMBER

September 5: Saint Teresa of Calcutta, Religious
1910–1997
Optional Memorial; Liturgical Color: White (Mother Teresa is not on the Church's universal calendar but is included here due to her renown)
Patron Saint of the Archdiocese of Calcutta, India

She equals in generosity the great 'Teresas' she emulated

Anjezë (Agnes) Gonxha Bojaxhiu was a tiny Albanian woman whose strong-as-iron faith served as a fulcrum to budge the world closer to God. She was born into a devout family in Skopje, in present day Macedonia. Her parent's marriage had been arranged, according to custom, and was happy and fruitful. The family was prosperous and regularly helped the poor and abandoned. There was seldom not a destitute person sharing the family table at lunchtime. Little Agnes benefited from the then recent reforms of Pope Saint Pius X lowering the age of First Holy Communion and thus received the Eucharist for the first time at the very young age of five and a half. After her father died young, Agnes' firm, loving, and religious mother had the greatest influence on her. The vibrant life of her local parish also impacted her faith. The priests there talked about the missionary work of the Church in far away lands, and Agnes internalized every word they spoke.

Feeling the call to serve Christ and the Church, Agnes decided to become a nun with the Loretto Sisters who were based in Dublin, Ireland. So when she was eighteen, a large procession of family, classmates, and parishioners accompanied her to Skopje's train station. After tender farewells, everyone wept and waved handkerchiefs as the train slowly pulled out of the station, and Agnes leaned out the window and wept and waved her handkerchief back at them until the train disappeared around a bend. Agnes would never see her beloved mother again. In the convent, Agnes chose the name Thérèse in honor of the Saint of Lisieux. But another nun had already chosen that name, so Agnes became Teresa, spelling the name in the Spanish style. After learning the Rule of her Order and basic English, she sailed on the long voyage to India, arriving in Calcutta in January 1929. India would be her home for the rest of her life.

SEPTEMBER

ST. MOTHER TERESA OF CALCUTTA
September 5

"If you're too busy to pray...you're too busy"

Sister Teresa taught at a girls' primary school in Calcutta, taking final vows in 1937, and was known warmly as Mother Teresa. Due to her open personality, self-discipline, deep prayer life, organizational abilities, and native intelligence, she became the school principal in 1944. Everyone loved her, especially her students, and Mother Teresa was a contented nun doing important work for the Church. Her youthful zeal had been fulfilled. But then something happened to alter her life's course, something entirely unexpected. In 1946, while riding on a train to her annual retreat, Mother Teresa received her "call within a call." Jesus told her, by mysterious means, that He desired her to serve Him in the poorest of the poor, who were so ignorant of Him and of His love. She must start a religious order.

Two years of organizing passed until, in August 1948, Mother Teresa donned her famous white and blue sari for the first time. She left the comfort and predictability of the Loretto convent school for a hard life on the street among the slums of the poorest, hungriest, and dirtiest people in Calcutta. Her order, the Missionaries of Charity, was formally established in 1950 and drew its first sisters from among Mother Teresa's former students. The order soon exploded with growth and expanded internationally. Missionaries of Charity sisters worked with AIDS patients, the dying, the starving, in soup kitchens, orphanages, and directly with the poor lying in filthy gutters.

By the time of her death in 1997, the Missionaries of Charity had over four thousand sisters serving in about one hundred and twenty countries. Mother Teresa became internationally famous, an icon of charity and peace, for all the right reasons. After her death it was revealed that she struggled to feel God's presence for much of her life but persevered in prayer and sacrifice nonetheless. She was constructed of steel, in perpetual motion, and operated on almost no food or sleep. All of her religious sisters are similarly indestructible. She was canonized by Pope Francis in 2016.

Saint Mother Teresa, your generosity to the poor and destitute inspired millions. Your life of dedication to prayer, to the Church, and to the dignity of all life inspires us still. May we emulate your life of total service and total love by loving God first.

SEPTEMBER

September 8: Birth of the Blessed Virgin Mary
Late First Century B.C.
Feast; Liturgical Color: White
Patroness of silversmiths, potters, and chefs

The last and greatest figure of the B.C. era causes its end

The birthdates of great men and women are remembered for posterity. The presidents of the United States are commemorated near the February birthday of George Washington. Many nations celebrate their birthday on the date they gained their independence. The Church celebrates its birthday, so to speak, on the Feast of Pentecost. However, the Church typically commemorates its saints on their date of death, ordination, or other significant milestone. Only Christ Himself, Saint John the Baptist, and the Virgin Mary have feasts commemorating their births, because only they were holy from the start. They were sanctified by God in the womb, not made holy through grace and long trial during their earthly lives.

Nowhere in Scripture is the place and date of birth of the Virgin Mary recorded. Nor are the names of her parents found in Scripture, although tradition tells us they were Joachim and Anne. It is not until the sixth century that there is certain knowledge of a liturgical commemoration of Mary's birth. This is not unusual. Mary lived a largely hidden life, and her theological and historical significance remained somewhat veiled until the Council of Ephesus in 431 formally declared her the Mother of God. Since that definition, every aspect of her life has become the source of a rich spiritual and theological heritage.

The Word of God, for the Catholic, is more than its written form. We are a people of the Word, not a people of the Book. Scripture is just one expression of the Word made flesh, the Word spoken by the Father from all ages. This means that a richer, more layered meaning of the events of the New Testament perpetually unfolds in the Church. The written Word of God in the Bible is limited by the fixed nature of all written words. Once put on paper, they don't change. The Living Word is something more, and it is the Living Word that the Church teaches, preaches, and lives. Just like a person, the Body of Christ expresses itself through both formal language and through body language. The words of the Catechism, prayers, and Magisterial documents use formal language. But the liturgy, sacraments, music, architecture, pious devotions, processions, etc., are more like body language. They communicate the same written truths as the Catechism and Scripture yet in a different, more corporeal, more lived way.

The silence of Mary, the hiddenness of so much of her life, is intriguing. It is an invitation to prayer and spiritual reflection. Her silence, and the silence of Scripture on so many events which must have occurred but are not referenced, means that there is, and will always be, more for the Church to reveal about Her greatest truths. It is not just Scripture that is inspired but the Church as well. She pulls from Her storehouse things old and new, polishes them off, and offers them to the faithful in culturally compelling language to deepen the content of faith and the faithful's response to it.

But even more than offering old things in new ways, even more than preserving past truths, the Church is a generator of revelation. She is the Living Word in the world of today, the vibrant Magisterium who absorbs the world's questions and challenges in every age and gives them compelling answers. Tradition for the Church, then, is not just a jewel to be guarded. Tradition is forward-looking, dynamic, and active. And this positive tradition continues to celebrate the birth of the Virgin Mary because it was she, the last great figure of the B.C. era, whose birth itself gave birth to a new world. No Mary, no Christ. Her birth was the start of the future we all now inhabit.

Saint Mary, we celebrate your holy birth in the land your Son made holy. Your discreet life of prayer and service obscures so much but speaks loudly as well. May our lives be discreet in their goodness, known to God and to those few who have the eyes to see and the ears to hear.

SEPTEMBER

September 9: Saint Peter Claver, Priest (U.S.A.)
1580–1654
Memorial; Liturgical Color: White
Patron Saint of slaves, Colombia, seafarers, and missionaries to Africa

A builder of the Spanish Bridge, he personified respect for human rights

It is commonly taught that human rights were born in the Anglo-Saxon Enlightenment of the seventeenth and eighteenth centuries. This thesis holds that non-Catholic, nominally Christian intellectuals, including the founders of the United States, were the first generation of thinkers to philosophically articulate, and legally protect, man's inherent, universal human rights. And, this train of thought concludes, these steps forward were possible only after the heavy chains of traditional Christianity fell to the ground. In other words, human rights were the obverse of Catholicism. As the shadow of the Church and its archaic teachings receded, the theory goes, the inherent dignity of individual man moved into the light. The problem with this thesis is twofold: first, it ignores one thousand seven hundred years of history; second, most Enlightenment thinkers owned other human beings just like they owned cows, or at least depended on the services of slaves or took advantage of slave women.

Today's saint was among numerous Spanish priests, nuns, and lay men and women who built the Spanish Bridge from the Old World to the New. They knew what Jesus taught. They internalized the content of the papal encyclicals condemning the indignity and immorality of slavery. They battled over human rights in royal courts, they risked life and limb confronting their own unscrupulous countrymen in the fields and ports of New Spain, and they sacrificed their personal health to care for slaves. Their intellectual advocacy for, and practical living out of, human rights is the true source of the Western world's embrace of human rights, not those few Anglo-Saxon intellectuals whose culture raised them to despise a broader tradition of which they were ignorant.

A converted former slave owner and fellow Spanish priest named Bartolomé de las Casas laid the intellectual groundwork for people like Peter Claver, today's saint. Claver practiced, in flesh and blood, what Las Casas had taught a few generations before him. Peter

SEPTEMBER

Claver *lived* human rights. He cared for actual persons at great cost to his own health. He did not write books like Las Casas or just give lip service to human dignity like many colonists. He implemented Catholic social teaching for over forty years, universalizing the concept of neighbor to include everyone, because everyone is made in God's image and likeness. He epitomized the sweet and sacrificial love of the Gospel of Jesus Christ.

Saint Peter Claver was from the region around Barcelona, Spain. He joined the Jesuits and requested to serve in the American missions. Like so many saints, when he left for God, he left for good. He never returned to friends and family in Spain. He was ordained a priest in the port city of Cartagena, Colombia, in 1615, and immediately and from then on dedicated himself to the physical and spiritual care of African slaves. But he didn't just care for them in the fields or plantations of Colombia. He met every slave ship he possibly could as soon as it dropped anchor in port. Using interpreters, he greeted the traumatized chained men and women with fresh water, ripe fruit, bandages, perfumes, food, medicine, lemons, a broad smile and charitable caresses. When weather prohibited seafaring and he didn't have to be in port, Peter instructed and baptized whatever slaves were open to it. He baptized more than forty thousand souls.

It is said that Saint Peter Claver lost his senses of taste and smell due to his long years of breathing obnoxious odors. He called himself the slave of the slaves. He also labored among the Spanish slave traders, attempting to convert them from their evil ways. When visiting his fellow Spaniards, he did not stay with them but in their often rancid slave quarters. This apostle of Cartagena died forgotten, alone, and poor. He was canonized in 1888.

Saint Peter Claver, you worked among the most traumatized and destitute populations of your time, caring for slaves, because they were made in the image and likeness of God. Help us to understand, protect, and exalt the inherent dignity of every human person, just like you did.

SEPTEMBER

ST. PETER CLAVER
September 9

"To love God as He ought to be loved, we must be detached from all temporal love. We must love nothing but Him, or if we love anything else, we must love it only for His sake."

SEPTEMBER

September 12: The Holy Name of the Blessed Virgin Mary

Optional Memorial; Liturgical Color: White

Every name begins a relationship

A name doesn't imply that you know everything about someone, but it does make a person "invocable." To know that there is a "someone" standing before you is not to know too much. When that "someone" has a name, however, he or she is placed in relationship with you, and relationships are what matter most. By means of a name, we go beyond a mere concept, beyond a mere thing. A name includes another in our circle of shared existence. No one wants to be a mere number, or to be just a "Nigerian," just an "athlete," or just an "accountant." Titles and monikers flatten people. They reduce someone to where they came from, what they excel at, their profession, their hair color, their language, and on and on. A name opens a door to the more complex reality that is every human soul.

The God of Christianity is not a mere concept who "does" but a being who "Is." He has a name. He is "Abba" or "Father." He is Jesus Christ. He is the Holy Spirit. It's hard to imagine truly knowing, or loving, a nameless entity whose identity is its function. We don't, after all, love "country." We love Poland, or the Philippines, or Bolivia. And we don't love "husband" or "wife," we love the concrete, specific, named person to whom we are married. Our love of God begins in the same way our love of people does—by asking His name.

Jesus Himself called out "Mary!" in the garden on the morning of His resurrection, and her spoken name elicited a beautiful response: "Rabboni!" In Chapter Three of the Book of Exodus, God calls Moses by name to approach Him in the burning bush. God first states that He is the God of Abraham, Isaac, and Jacob. But Moses is not completely satisfied with knowing *that* God is, or *for whom* He is. So Moses asks the question everyone asks when they want to deepen a relationship: "What's your name?" God then pulls the curtains aside and invites Moses into His inner life, into relationship with Him. He reveals something more intimate. He tells Moses His name—"Yahweh" or "I am Who I Am." God hands over part of

Himself to man. He can now be called upon. He is invocable. No one can force you to reveal your name. It's personal, because to reveal your name is to become vulnerable.

Today the Church commemorates a name as much as the person who bears it. The holiness of the name of God, which the Second Commandment forbids man to take in vain, is reflected in the holy names of all the saints and holy things and holy places dedicated to Him. The name of the Mother of God, the Holy or Blessed Virgin Mary, should be safe in our mouths. This feast falls during the Octave of the Birthday of the Virgin Mary and was inserted into the Church's universal calendar just after the triumph of the Christian army over the Turks at the Battle of Vienna in 1683. The feast was suppressed after Vatican II but once again placed in the calendar by Pope Saint John Paul II in 2002.

Mary's name evokes tenderness and maternity. All Christians should call upon the blessed name of the Mother of God as the most powerful intercessor before the throne of Her Son in heaven. Her name puts us in relationship with her. She is not far away. She is close to us, as a mother should be, and she wants to be called upon by her children who are so in need of her.

Saint Mary, may your holy name be always respected and honored, because you are closer to God than we are, because you know Him more intimately than we do, and because we trust that you will be with us now and at the hour of our death. Amen.

September 13: Saint John Chrysostom, Bishop and Doctor
c. 347–407
Memorial; Liturgical Color: White
Patron Saint of preachers and speakers

A great preacher, writer, and intellectual suffers for the faith

In the tug and pull of the theological disputes of the fourth and fifth centuries, today's saint was a seminal figure. Along with other luminaries such as Saints Ambrose, Athanasius, Hilary, Basil and many others, he tunneled deep into Scripture and the existing Christian tradition to carve out what is today known as the deposit of faith. Saint John Chrysostom was from Antioch, that "Metropolis of heresy" in Saint John Henry Newman's words, where Arianism was bred, incubated, thrived, and died in the period between the Council of Nicea in 325 and the Council of Constantinople in 381.

John received an excellent education in the liberal arts and was baptized at the age of eighteen, in keeping with the custom of adult baptism common to his era. He joined a rustic group of hermits in the hills outside of his hometown in his mid-twenties. The conditions were so physically and psychologically brutal, though, that he left after seven years. Living always isolated and mortified would not be his path. He was ordained a priest in 386. His bishop recognized his gifts and put him in charge of the physical and pastoral care of the poor of Antioch, a ministry in which he honed his natural gifts as a preacher. He was so skillful in preaching that he was given, a century after his death, the title of *chrysostom* or "golden mouth." John's theological acumen was no less impressive. His sermons and letters display a refined understanding of the intricacies of the Holy Trinity and of the Gospels. His beautiful theological and spiritual reflections are referenced numerous times in the modern Catechism of the Catholic Church.

In 398 Saint John was consecrated the Archbishop of Constantinople, the New Rome, provoking jealousy among some contemporaries. John did himself no favors by his overaggressive reforms as Archbishop. He bluntly criticized women for wearing make-up, Christians for attending races and games on holy days, the imperial court for its extravagances, and the clergy for their laxity and wealth-seeking. Recriminations soon followed. He was falsely charged with treason and other crimes and was exiled in 402. He was reinstated after an earthquake in Constantinople was interpreted as divine punishment for his banishment. But John was exiled a second time shortly thereafter. Like other saints, his time of exile proved fruitful. He wrote numerous letters, specifically to bishops in the Western Empire, including the pope. But also like other exiled popes and bishops, assertions of support were only as sturdy as the paper on which they were written. Practical help never materialized.

John died in exile in 407, a victim of cold, rain, a forced march and lack of food. Within a decade after his death, his reputation was restored by the pope, and his remains were transferred for burial in

Constantinople. He was recognized as a Father of the Church at the Council of Chalcedon in 451 and declared a Doctor of the Church in 1568.

Saint John suffered for his zeal. He was exiled by civil power in an age when correct theology was understood as a form of patriotism, and heresy as treason. He crossed the civil powers of his age, did not back down, and paid a severe price for his fidelity. When Crusaders sacked Constantinople in 1204, they stole John's relics and carried them back to Rome. In 2004 Pope Saint John Paul II authorized the return of some of John's remains to the seat of the Orthodox Patriarch in Saint George Church in present-day Istanbul, John's own episcopal city.

Saint John Chrysostom, the heat of your words burned so hot that you were persecuted for your ardor. Inspire all Christian preachers to light a fire of faith in their congregations, without fear for their own reputations or of recrimination.

September 14: Exaltation of the Holy Cross

Feast; Liturgical Color: Red
Patronal Feast of Cortona, Italy

A torture device is transformed into a universal symbol of hope and peace

If the Romans had hung criminals from a gibbet, then Catholic churches would display a noose in their sanctuaries instead of a cross. Or a statue of Jesus' lifeless body would be hanging in the sanctuary from a sturdy branch with a rope wrapped tightly around His neck. If the Romans had practiced stoning as their chosen form of capital punishment, then there would be a pile of rocks for the congregation to gaze at in hope, with Jesus' body, bruised and broken, lying lifeless nearby. We are accustomed to the cross. We wear it around our necks, chisel it onto our tombstones, tattoo it onto our arms, and anchor it into rocky mountain peaks. We even top our steeples with the cross and illuminate it at night. The Church has been so spectacularly successful in communicating its truths about suffering and death, about resurrection and life, that we perhaps don't notice that, over long centuries, a device of torture and death has been reinterpreted as the world's greatest symbol of life and peace.

This is the paradox of the cross. Today's feast commemorates the Cross because in spiritual combat with life, the cross lost. A conqueror might plant the head of his decapitated opponent on a spike, a soldier might return from a far-away war with an enemies' flag captured in the heat of battle, or an American Indian might tuck the scalps of his poor victims under his saddle. Trophies of war take many forms. The Cross is Christ's war trophy. The Church exalts the Cross on this liturgical feast because this enemy of life was felled like timber by the Son of God. The Cross was brought low and humbled. It was mocked when Jesus rose from the dead. The Church holds up the Cross to say "Behold what the cross did not do. Behold that life conquers even a cruel and public death."

God's self-emptying started at the incarnation. He humbled himself to walk among us when He restricted Himself to the limitations of His own creatures. God continued to pour Himself out until He climbed onto the wood of the Cross, completing the total self-gift that was His life. Our God is not like a general who sends a subordinate to carry out a dangerous mission, like an absent parent who pays someone else to raise his children, or like a physician who coldly touches his patient's body and then washes in antiseptic. No, our God is like a surgeon who, before he cuts, points to his side and says to the patient with empathy, "I had the same—see my scars." Our God points to the wound in His open side and says, "I too was the victim of evil and death." God bore the Cross and its cruel death so that He could drink from the same bitter cup as man, so that He could enter more fully into the world's sorrow.

Death on the Cross was not preordained. God could have freely chosen other ways to redeem the human race—through intelligence, wisdom, charm, money, or education. But then, to participate in His redemption, we would have to study for a PhD, attend etiquette school, get a good job, earn an excellent wage, or receive good grades. Not everyone can do these things. But everyone *can* die. Death is egalitarian. Everyone does it, eventually. So God did it and "so made the grave a sign of hope that promises resurrection even as it claims our mortal bodies," as the graveside prayer states. The Cross, then, is everyone's trophy, raised high with one arm, head cocked to the side. It is in this sense that the Cross is a sign of hope. Because the Cross lost the fight with Christ, death is not the final answer. The Cross says that our God does not answer the question of suffering and death in a partial academic way. He responds in a total human way. He responds with His life. He doesn't explain; He shares. He responds with empathy by taking up His Cross and inviting us to do the same.

Jesus Christ, Your three hours on the Cross gave that wicked device a new meaning. Through contemplation of Your sufferings, may we transform all the wickedness and sin in our lives into something valuable. May we convert evil, transform sin, and, like You, go from death to life.

September 15: Our Lady of Sorrows

Memorial; Liturgical Color: White
Patroness of Slovakia

A mother is only as happy as her saddest child

Every life climbs its Calvary. Every soul has its quiet sorrow which cannot be shared in full with any other soul. This concealed pain is the very real drama that plays out behind the curtain of the duties and distractions of everyday life. Jesus Christ, fully God and fully man, shared in all things human, save sin, including pain and sorrow. So He wept at the death of Lazarus, and He balanced the heavy cross on His sore bones and trudged up a hill to His own execution. Thoughts and ideas can be shared in their totality. Emotions and experiences only partially so. Suffering is intensely private in that it is a personal, lived experience. The intense sufferings of Jesus Christ were intensified by His perfection. It was more unjust, more cruel, that one so perfect should suffer at the hands of creatures of His own making. Only a perfect being similar to Jesus could enter into His sorrow, could experience it somewhat as He did. That person was Mary. She was not a Goddess, of course, but the New Eve, the perfect person God intended that every person should be from the start. Because she was perfect, she most understood, and felt, the pain of her perfect Son. Shared perfection led to shared sorrow.

Today's feast commemorates the sorrows of Mary, most especially those lived during Jesus' passion and death. Devotional images of

Mary show her heart pierced by seven swords, symbolic of seven sorrows: the prophecy of Simeon; the flight into Egypt; Jesus being lost in the temple; meeting Jesus on His way to Calvary; standing at the foot of the Cross; being present when Jesus was removed from the Cross; and her presence at His burial. Mary was perfect, but her life wasn't perfect. She was squeezed by the same wine press of pain, humiliation, and sorrow that squeezes every life. She was unmarried and pregnant and must have heard the neighbors' whispers as she walked the dusty streets of her town. She and her family had to flee to a far-off land to escape the murderous King Herod the Great. She lived a real life stuffed with real human drama. But her most intense sorrows were felt when she was in her late forties, when her one and only child died a public death, leaving her, already a widow, totally alone, her middle-aged face stretched with sorrow.

When our fingers and thumb walk up and down the chain of God's mercy, we ruminate over things glorious, joyful, luminous, and sorrowful. We recall historical events like Christ's Baptism and the Last Supper, and theological events like the Assumption and the Coronation. The Sorrowful Mysteries are historical. Mary hovers just off center stage. She stands nearby, amidst the crowd on the path to Calvary, upright and brave at the foot of the Cross, weeping as her dead boy is wrapped in a sheet and delicately placed on a cold slab in a rock-cut tomb. She is Our Lady of Sorrows because she, and the Church, are mothers. They give and nurture life. They feel more than men. They respond to suffering with co-suffering, not so much through actions and solutions. On today's feast, we recall Mary's sorrow and share in it. But our sorrow is not that of a godless Viking, a pagan Roman, or a modern secularist. Christian grief is not godless grief. Our grief, like Mary's grief, is ameliorated by the sure and certain hope that the last word in our book is not death and despair but hope and life. Mary's sorrow is temporary, as all of our sorrows one day will be. There is nothing that does not have a context, except for God. And the context for Christian sorrow is the Resurrection.

Mary of Sorrows, you shared the pain and sorrow of your perfect Son but were never forlorn. Help all who turn to you to unite our sorrows to yours and His so that we may co-suffer in His death and co-share in His Resurrection.

September 16: Saint Cornelius, Pope, Martyr
c. Late Second, or Early Third, Century–253
Memorial; Liturgical Color: Red
Patron Saint of cattle, domestic animals, and earache sufferers

A Pope reigns for two years, excommunicates a schismatic, and dies in exile

The twenty-first pope of the Church, Saint Cornelius, succeeded no one. After the death of Pope Saint Fabian, martyred in January 250, persecutions prohibited the clergy of Rome from electing a successor, so the Chair of Saint Peter was vacant for over a year. Finally, when the cruel Emperor Decius departed Rome on military campaign, the clergy chose Cornelius as Bishop of Rome. Not everyone was happy with the choice, especially the former future pope Novatian, who had led the Roman clergy during the vacancy and had convinced himself that he was going to be elected. Novatian's supporters consecrated him bishop and refused to acknowledge Cornelius. Sides were taken, letters were written, and tensions heightened. After consolidating support from the esteemed Saint Cyprian, Bishop of Carthage, and others, Cornelius resolved the dispute by convening a synod of bishops which excommunicated the schismatic Novatian and his followers.

Pope Cornelius reigned for a little over two years, from March 251 to June 253. Even though his time in office was brief, he made some important decisions and left an interesting legacy. Decius' persecution gave rise to the greatest pastoral dilemma of the third century—how, and whether, to reintegrate Christians who had offered pagan sacrifice, regretted it, and desired to enter again into the embrace of Mother Church. The related question of whether bishops, priests, and deacons who had apostatized could perform valid sacraments would vex Cornelius's successors. There were two camps on this issue. Novatian held that lapsed Christians were idolaters, and idolatry was, in the Old Testament especially, unforgivable. The Church could not absolve such apostates. They were to be judged by God alone at death. Cornelius, Saint Cyprian, and other bishops occupied a more moderate position. They taught that the *lapsi* could be reintegrated into the Church through repentance and an appropriate penance. Cornelius' position won the day, forever and always, establishing an important theological precedent: There is no sin that cannot be forgiven.

Pope Cornelius also left, in his letters, an important record of the size, state, and organization of the Church of Rome, hard facts so obvious to those inside of a culture that they often go unreported

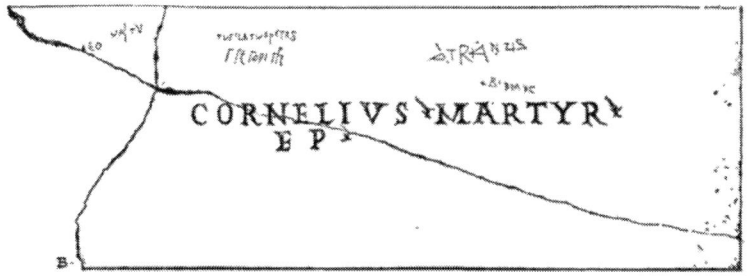

Tombstone of Pope St. Cornelius

in historical documents. Decius' successor as Emperor was named Gallus, and he was no friend of Christians either. He banished Cornelius to a city not far from Rome where the Pope died of physical hardship. Saint Cornelius was buried near the papal crypt in the Catacombs of Saint Callixtus. One day in 1849, an amateur archeologist, a layman who worked in the Vatican library, found a small marble shard that read NELIUS MARTYR in a field on the outskirts of Rome. But there was no martyr named Nelius. He then found another shard that read COR. The inscription is still visible today in the Catacombs of Callixtus: Cornelius Martyr.

The Romans unsheathed their long knives in the 250s. Pope after pope was martyred by various means. But the Church did not run and hide, it stayed and grew. The blood of Cornelius and other pope-martyrs wet the soil, and the seeds of faith moistened, grew, and sprouted into the vast garden of Catholicism that slowly, and imperceptibly, took deep root in the ground of Europe. Saint Cornelius' name is read at Mass in Eucharistic Prayer I even today, next to Saint Cyprian's. He was staunch in his defense of the Church, yet appropriately lenient to his fellow Christians who did not possess his same fortitude. In this respect, he was as wise a pastor as he was brave a martyr.

Saint Cornelius, our Lord said that it profits a man nothing to gain the whole world if he would lose his own soul. You gained the papacy, not the whole world, yet gave it up rather than bend to the will of the Church's enemies. Help us to persevere like you.

September 16: Saint Cyprian, Bishop, Martyr
c.200–258
Memorial; Liturgical Color: Red
<u>Patron Saint of Algeria and North Africa</u>

The faithful soak up the blood of their beheaded bishop

The elegantly named Thaschus Caecilius Cyprianus was born in an uncertain year in that buzzing beehive of early Christianity known as Roman North Africa. His biography epitomizes that of many greats of his era: a classically educated Roman citizen of renown finds Christ as an adult, leaves behind his exalted civic status, trades Empire for Church, and places his gifts and reputation at the service of the people as a bishop of consequence. But because he lived in times of hot persecution, Cyprian's life did not come to a peaceful end like others with similar biographies, such as Saints Hilary, Ambrose, Augustine, or Paulinus of Nola. The mighty Bishop Cyprian was sentenced to death by a local bureaucrat. On the fateful day, he knelt in the burning sand and waited for the heavy Roman sword to lop off his head. Cyprian's cult of martyrdom sprang up instantly, even as the faithful, carrying white cloths, soaked up the holy blood that dripped from his torso. His name was soon placed in the Roman Canon, where it remains today, spoken from the altar and heard by the faithful at Mass in Eucharistic Prayer I.

Cyprian was a big-hearted, well-educated "man about town" when, in his mid-forties, he was converted by the example and words of an old priest. He redirected his life, made a vow of chastity that astonished his friends, and even abstained from his greatest pleasure—the works of pagan authors. In all of Cyprian's Christian writings, there is not one single citation of these pagans whose style and thought Cyprian had so admired. Once converted, Cyprian's mind focused on Scripture and the growing canon of Christian theology, mostly that of his fellow North African Tertullian. Soon after his baptism, Cyprian was ordained a priest, and in 248, after first resisting the appointment, he was made the bishop of his home city of Carthage. His impressive bearing and refined education earned him deep respect among the faithful. His biographer, a deacon named Pontus, wrote about Cyprian precisely so that the great man would be known for the example of his entire life, not just his last few heroic moments.

Under the persecution of the Emperor Decius (249–252), which so marked the life of the third-century Church, many Christians lined up at the office of their local Roman official to offer token worship to pagan gods and to receive a *libellus*, or small sheet, documenting their apostasy. Cyprian lost all his possessions in this persecution but avoided capture by going into hiding. He governed his diocese remotely through letters. He was also compelled to defend his flight against criticism levelled by bishops in both Rome and North Africa that he was avoiding martyrdom. Once the tide of persecution subsided, Cyprian returned to Carthage and was lenient but clear, like his contemporary Pope Cornelius, in reintegrating the *lapsi* back into the Church once they had performed a suitable penance.

The roiling debate over how to pastorally respond to the *lapsi* divided the Church in North Africa, with some priests arguing no forgiveness was possible for idolaters, and others demanding that the *lapsi* perform onerous penances before they were received again into the fold. Cyprian responded to these divisions by writing a treatise on Church unity, arguing that the Pope's teaching on this matter must be obeyed: "There is one God, one Christ, and but one episcopal chair, originally founded on Peter, by the Lord's authority.

There cannot be set up another altar or another priesthood." Cyprian later clashed with Pope Stephen I over the validity of the sacraments performed by priests who had apostatized, a matter resolved after both mens' death in favor of the Roman position of leniency.

Cyprian's fellow North African, Saint Augustine of Hippo, in Book Five of his Confessions, recounts how his mother, Monica, prayed in a shrine dedicated to Saint Cyprian in the port city of Carthage around 375 A.D. So, approximately one hundred and twenty years after Cyprian's death, his legacy was firmly established, fresh and alive, as it still is today.

Saint Cyprian, you served the unity of the Church as a bishop, understood the beauty and necessity of the sacraments, and accepted death over apostasy. Inspire all bishops to be magnets, drawing the faithful toward Christ and the Church through their teaching and witness.

September 17: Saint Robert Bellarmine, Bishop and Doctor
1542–1621
Optional Memorial; Liturgical Color: White
Patron Saint of catechists and catechumens

A learned scholar with a warm personality drives the Counter-Reformation forward

A massive, multi-volume work of Christian theology was published in the 1580s refuting Protestant errors. The volumes were of such encyclopedic and commanding erudition that readers assumed that the name on the books' spines, "Bellarmine," referred to an entire faculty of scholars. But the volumes were the work of just one incredible man, today's saint, Robert Bellarmine. He was a one-man university. The Bellarmines had a pope in the family and gave their son a broad education from his youth. Young Robert mastered numerous subjects, including the art of playing the violin. He joined the Jesuits in 1560 and taught the classics while simultaneously studying theology on his path to the Priesthood. After his ordination in 1570, he became a professor at the University of Louvain, in modern-day Belgium, and then at the Jesuit College in Rome.

During his long career as a professor, Father Bellarmine never stopped learning. He was rigorous in his intellectual approach, read everything, and was particularly focused on refuting, with nuance, Protestant errors. He even learned Hebrew and wrote a Hebrew grammar to counter the thesis of a then popular Protestant history book. The times demanded that Bellarmine develop an expertise in apologetics, to be totally engaged with the red-hot controversies of his day. This was not the age for theological speculation or philosophical rumination, as the medieval scholastics could indulge in. This was the age to master first principles, to delve into the ancient sources, to root out error, and to express the perennial truths of Catholicism with renewed vigor surrounded by new art, architecture, and sacred music. It was a total mind-body approach. It was the Baroque exploding before your eyes. It was the onslaught of the Counter-Reformation, and Robert Bellarmine was the tip of the spear.

Bellarmine's long list of accomplishments is astonishing. He helped produce a new edition of Saint Jerome's Vulgate Bible, participated in the revision of the Julian calendar, and contributed to the authoritative Catechism which the Church published for over three hundred years. He served on a papal commission that arbitrated a major conflict over the Kingship of France, became a regional superior for the Jesuits, and was ordained a bishop and consecrated a Cardinal. He was a trusted adviser to successive popes, was tasked with resolving a bitter dispute over the theology of grace between Dominicans and Jesuits, and escaped being elected Pope himself by the narrowest of margins in 1605. After this near miss with destiny, he was appointed to serve on various Roman Congregations and as prefect of the Vatican library, so he resigned from his diocesan responsibilities and returned to Rome for the rest of his life, where he became the Holy See's indispensable man. His long and faithful service at the highest levels of the Church culminated in his playing a role in the famous process against Galileo, who was Bellarmine's personal friend. Our saint's last years were spent writing devotional works on prayer and dying well.

Robert Bellarmine accepted the trappings of his office—robes, servants, and a carriage—but he lived austerely and expected all priests to do the same. His virtues equaled his achievements. He had an attractive blend of warmth, intelligence, and big-heartedness that earned him a huge circle of friends. He knew the truth like few others but listened carefully and respectfully to all who challenged it. Robert Bellarmine was canonized in 1930 and declared a Doctor of the Church in 1931. He is buried in the Jesuit Church of Saint Ignatius in Rome.

Saint Robert Bellarmine, we see in your life a beautiful dedication to theological truth, personal austerity, and openness toward others. We ask your intercession before God to give all the faithful the gift to live so balanced and integrated a life.

September 17: Saint Hildegard of Bingen, Virgin and Doctor
1098-1179
Optional Memorial; Liturgical Color: White
Patroness of philologists

A one-woman magisterium orchestrates a life in tune with the Creator

In the high Middle-Ages, she was New-Age. Before farm-to-table was a term, she lived organically. Before alternative medicine was *de rigueur*, she catalogued the medicinal benefits of herbs, plants, minerals, and potions. And before anyone ever "went green" to save planet earth, she talked about the "viriditas," or greenness, of God, meaning how His graces watered a desiccated soul until it flowered with fresh, green, life. Hildegard of Bingen was far, far, ahead of her time even though, from an external perspective, she lived the austere, rigorous, cloistered life common to the female religious of her era.

Hildegard was born in the Rhineland, the very western region of modern Germany, to a minor noble family. Her mother and father placed her in the care of a well-known local abbess for her education at the tender age of eight, where she learned Latin and the teachings of the Catholic religion. Her world deepened and broadened inside the four walls of her simple Benedictine convent. When her mentor died, Hildegard became the abbess and soon moved the convent, generating some tension in the process, to a new location where it could better flourish as her fame attracted more and more notice and vocations.

Hildegard was unusual for her time. She was unusual, in fact, for any time. She was a polymath with eclectic interests in numerous fields of study. She was a sophisticated and prolific composer of sacred music whose voluminous works surpass the output of almost any other Mediaeval musician. She had an advanced understanding of medicine and the human body, including an almost complete knowledge of how blood circulated in the body - four centuries before such knowledge was verified through post-mortem studies. Hildegard also had detailed knowledge of animal and plant life, of rocks, reptiles, fish, and the natural sciences in general.

Yet if she must be known for one thing above all, it must be for her pyrotechnic visions of God and the cosmos. Hildegard's colorful visions are difficult to classify. She described them as a wide-awake spiritual awareness of the "reflection of the living light." From childhood, she felt her entire body – bones, nerves, veins, senses – all rising ever higher into the vault of heaven where she experienced all of creation in its particularity and in its oneness. These were not ecstasies or physical transportations, but an eyes-wide-open, all-sensory experience of sermons, virtues, writings, and other human actions as if they were shimmering like the sun on the mirror-like surface of a lake. The over-arching theme of these visions was the mystical marriage between God and His creation through the incarnation of Jesus Christ, a union consummated on the cross, where Christ makes his Bride, the Church, fertile for humanity.

As Hildegard's writings became more well-known, the Pope was asked for his appreciation of their theological orthodoxy or heterodoxy. Pope Eugene III approved of Hildegarde's description of her visions, with a prudent warning for Hildegard to avoid any pride in being so blessed. The great St. Bernard of Clairvaux, a famous contemporary of Hildegard, was also asked his opinions about her writings and the two exchanged letters. In fact, many people, both humble and exalted, corresponded with Hildegard, leaving behind one of the most massive caches of extant letters from mediaeval times.

In the last years of her life, despite worsening health, Hildegarde's prestige was such that she was given permission to leave her convent in order to preach in town squares and Churches, something almost unheard of for a woman of her era. She died in the odor of sanctity on September 17, 1179, the day on which her liturgical memorial is celebrated today. In the 2012 Papal Bull declaring her a Doctor of the Church, Pope Benedict XVI wrote that "the corpus of her writings, for their quantity, quality and variety of interests, is unmatched by any other female author of the Middle Ages."

Saint Hildegarde, your creative and versatile soul brought a feminine genius to the Church's theological and spiritual patrimony, using poetic and symbolic language to express the mysterious richness of God and his creation. Inspire all Christians to read creation like a book of divine life.

September 19: Saint Januarius, Bishop and Martyr
c. 300
Optional Memorial; Liturgical Color: Red
Patron Saint of Naples

An early bishop martyr is honored due to an enduring miracle of blood

In every lost corner and hidden valley of the Catholic world is a painting of the Virgin Mary that cries watery tears, a crucifix whose growing hair must be cut with scissors, a white host oozing drops of red blood, or a sacred pool whose baths make the blind see and the lame walk. Of all the miracles, wonders, and theological rarities that leave God's family in awe, the miracle of today's saint is one of the most astounding. Three times a year—on his day of martyrdom, September 19; on the day of his commemoration as Patron of Naples, December 16; and on the Saturday before the first Sunday of May, recalling the gathering together of his various relics—the blood of Saint Januarius liquefies.

Since at least the 1300s, a small glass vial holding a deep-red, stable substance has been removed from a safe location and brought before the faithful in the Cathedral of Naples by a priest or bishop. The vial is placed near the other relics of Saint Januarius which rest under the altar. And then the drumbeat of prayers start. They sometimes continue for hours and sometimes for minutes. God is bidden, fuel is poured on the fire of faith, and the mysterious moment arrives. Spontaneously, the stable, solid, red substance is transformed into a liquid that splashes around the inside walls of the vial for all to see. The blood of Saint Januarius has come to life.

The city of Naples fires a twenty-one-gun salute from a nearby castle to signal that the transformation has occurred.

There is no explanation for how this happens. But it happens, happens often, and has happened consistently for many centuries. The proof is the outcome itself. That a solid substance liquifies cannot be debated. The liquified blood must be the starting point for speculation, not a presumption of magic or sleight of hand. That some things of God cannot be explained without the informed trust of faith is simply to state that believers did not make God up. He is not understandable. If He were, then He would fit conveniently into our tiny brains and thus not be God. But no faith is needed to accept this miracle. What happens is a fact.

Little is known about the life of Saint Januarius. An extant letter from 432 mentions him as if he were already well known. It states that a nearby bishop, a friend of Saint Augustine named Saint Paulinus of Nola, had a vision of Januarius just before Paulinus died, and that Januarius was a bishop and martyr and a well-known member of the Church of Naples. It is believed that our saint was beheaded during a persecution under the reign of Diocletian, in the decade before Christianity was legalized in the early 300s.

Perhaps the most interesting thing about the liquifying of Saint Januarius' blood is that it occurs for no specific purpose. No sick person is healed, no sacrament is celebrated, no bishop is elected. It is a divine folly. It occurs to edify, to entertain, and to inspire, as if religion were a theological sport, with God simply putting His talents on display for all to behold the spectacle from the pews, to gaze, mouth agape, at a wonder that can neither be explained nor be resisted.

Saint Januarius, you died for the faith of the Church just as the Christian era dawned. May we follow your example of generous witness and stand astonished at the mysterious miracle that puts your name on so many lips so many centuries after you perished for Christ.

SEPTEMBER

September 20: Andrew Kim Tae-gŏn, Priest, and Paul Chŏng Ha-sang, and Companions, Martyrs

Nineteenth century
Memorial; Liturgical Color: Red
Patron Saints of Korea

Their martyrdom for a new faith caused the Christian sun to rise in Korea

Catholicism was not originally brought to the isolated Korean Peninsula by celibate missionaries who trekked over its remote borders or who landed on its far shores from the outside. Instead, native Korean intellectuals had heard interesting ideas and had read intriguing books imported from nearby China about a new faith. These diplomats, professors and poets went in search of the Church. They crossed their own borders to speak with Jesuit priests in Beijing. The Koreans dialogued with the Jesuits, read their works, witnessed the celebration of the sacraments, and saw the Chinese Church in action. One of these Korean scholars, a man named Yi-Sung-hun, was baptized as Peter in Beijing in 1784 by a French missionary. Newly minted in Christ, with a convert's fervor, Peter filled his baggage with catechisms, crucifixes, statues, rosaries, and images of the Virgin Mary and headed back to Korea excited to unpack the new faith for all to see. Peter baptized some of his friends and together they formed the first community of Catholics in Korea. They met in a house where sits, today, the Cathedral of Myeongdong.

The evangelization of Korea dawned as a thoroughly lay initiative. And once the Catholic seed was planted in Korean soil, it first grew slowly among scholars but then more steadily among the larger populace over time. Today's feast commemorates the official persecution that burned hot, then cold, then hot, for decades as those first Christian seeds germinated. As the Church grew like a plant, it protruded too high over the land and was repeatedly cut down in the bloody harvest commemorated today. Hundreds of martyrs, mostly lay men and women, but some French missionary bishops and priests as well, were murdered by successive Korean governments throughout the last decade of the eighteenth century

SEPTEMBER

and throughout the nineteenth for the crime of being baptized Catholics. They posed no other threat.

Paul Chŏng Ha-sang was a nobleman whose father and brother were martyred. Sacrifice was in his genes. Paul traveled to Beijing nine times, pleading for the Chinese Church to send priests to the lay-led Korean Church. Along with others, he sent a letter to Pope Pius VII describing the plight of the Korean faithful. Once clandestine priests began to arrive regularly in the 1830s, Paul would go to the Korean border to escort them to the communities of the faithful and lodge them in his own home. Paul was executed in 1839. His mother and sister were killed shortly after him.

Father Andrew Kim Tae-gŏn was the very first native-born Korean priest. He departed Korea in 1837 for the Portuguese settlement of Macau to complete his seminary studies. He was ordained by a French missionary bishop in Shanghai in August 1845. He then guided back to Korea the same bishop and a French priest. His priestly ministry would be to die. He was arrested less than a year after his ordination. The authorities were so impressed with his personal bearing, education, and linguistic abilities that they agonized over whether he should be executed. They wrestled with their consciences, but their consciences, in the end, lost. Father Andrew was beheaded at the age of twenty-six in September 1846.

The struggle to establish an organized Church structure in Korea was brutal. Today's martyrs, whose names are all known and about whom basic facts are verified, stand in the fore. Yet behind them stand, faceless and nameless, thousands of other martyrs known to God alone. They perished by the sword, by crucifixion, in prison, or of starvation, rather than renounce their Christian faith when faced with certain torture and death. The Catholic Church in South Korea today is immense and vibrant, fully Korean and fully Catholic. The Church in North Korea does not effectively exist, and martyrs may still be dying there today, squeezed to death in the iron grip of its dictators. The story of the Korean Church is one of daring, one of steely courage, but one of tears. Only in 1886 did the century of persecution end, with a French-Korean treaty. Pope Saint John Paul II canonized Father Andrew Kim, Paul Chŏng Ha-sang,

ST. ANDREW KIM TAE-GŎN
September 20

"This is my last hour of life, listen to me attentively...My immortal life is on the point of beginning. Become Christians if you wish to be happy after death, because God has eternal chastisements in store for those who have refused to know Him."

and 101 other Korean martyrs on May 6, 1984, at a Mass in Seoul, South Korea. It was, at that time, the largest gathering of humanity in the history of the Korean peninsula. The martyrs' blood was fertile.

Holy Korean martyrs, known and unknown, we implore your powerful intercession in heaven. Give us half your courage, a quarter of your daring, and just one percent of your faith. With that we can emulate you in the easy circumstances of today, where we suffer metaphorically, but rarely in our bodies.

September 21: Saint Matthew, Apostle and Evangelist
First Century
Feast; Liturgical Color: Red
Patron Saint of bankers, accountants, and money changers

A lover of money becomes greedy for God

People leave their jobs for all sorts of reasons: more pay, better opportunity, a shorter commute. Today's saint left his job for a better boss. Matthew was at work in the city of Capernaum, a bustling town with a customs house. It was just another day, and Matthew was going about his job of collecting taxes. Nearby, Jesus was doing his job too, curing a paralyzed man. It was an ordinary day for both of them. But after performing His miracle, Jesus walked down the main street of Capernaum, saw Matthew outside of the customs house, and then...the normal day ended. Jesus said to Matthew, simply, directly, and with force, "Follow me." And then something astonishing happened. Matthew followed Him. Fistfuls of Roman coins may have spilled from his hands, or he may have swallowed a gulp in his throat, quickly adjusted his tunic, and then scurried to walk in the small clouds of dust that puffed up behind Jesus as His sandals slapped the dry ground. In an instant, Matthew's life changed forever and always. He had become a follower, a joiner, of the most important man in the history of the world.

The Gospel of Matthew nowhere mentions that it is written by a man named Matthew. But it was attributed to him very early in the life of the Church. It was compiled by 80 A.D., at the latest. Matthew's Gospel is clearly written by a Jew and for Jews. It references the Old Testament repeatedly and notes how Jesus fulfilled those ancient Scriptures. Matthew's Gospel is the only one which identifies him as a tax collector. Mark and Luke refer to him as Levi, which may have been his birth name, while Matthew ("gift of Yahweh") was his post-conversion name. Because it begins with a genealogy, Matthew's Gospel, but not Matthew himself, is in art represented by a man or by a man's face. After his big moment in Capernaum, Matthew's name consistently appears in the Gospels' lists of Apostles, but little more is said about him, apart from a feast he hosts in honor of Jesus. It is not known where he evangelized or where or how he died. Four churches in France alone claim to have Matthew's head, implying that no one has his head.

Christ passes by in every life. Everyone has their chance to say "Yes" or "No," to stay or follow, to change or remain the same. That moment may come only once and never return. Sudden callings, and sudden conversions, are rare, but they do happen. A life is more likely to plot gradually up or down like a line on a graph than to take a sharp right angle in either direction. Matthew's life angled sharply when his personal trajectory intersected with Christ's. The moment is captured in all of its drama by the painter Caravaggio in his *Calling of Saint Matthew*. A broad shaft of light beams through the room from above Christ's head. His bony finger points to a well-dressed man at a table with his hands over a pile of coins. The scene unfolds not in the street but in a darkened room. Light and darkness play. Sin and virtue tussle. Past, present, and future hang in the balance. Christ seems to say, "Will you take and eat, will you go and sell, will you come and follow me?" Difficult, challenging questions. But Matthew gave the difficult, generous answer in response, and we remember him today due to that one moment.

Saint Matthew, you made the right decision at the right time and so changed your life and those of millions of others who know Christ because of you. Help us to recognize when a pivot point arrives in our own life, when we must change direction, and help us to choose that direction well.

SEPTEMBER

September 23: Saint Pio of Pietrelcina (Padre Pio), Priest
1887–1968
Memorial; Liturgical Color: White
Patron Saint of civil defense volunteers and adolescents

A humble friar's love for Christ burns holes in his hands

Long-married spouses often develop similar patterns of speech. A boy might learn to walk just like his father, and a girl might favor the same hairstyle as her mom. Teenagers in the same cliques dress alike and cut their hair in a similar fashion. It is natural to adopt the traits of the one you love, to mimic their behavior, dress, speech, and habits, consciously or unconsciously. Lover and beloved converge, master and disciple unite, leader and follower bond. Today's saint did not have a reference group apart from Christ Himself. Jesus Christ inhabited every corner of the mind, soul, and imagination of Saint Pio of Pietrelcina. Pio's life fused with Christ's so totally that Pio's very body bore the marks of his beloved. Not the same haircut, clothes, or gait, but the same nail marks and bloody wounds. Father Pio merged with Christ such that to look upon the friar's hands was to see the crucified palms of the Son of God on Calvary.

Padre Pio grew up dirt poor and uneducated in a village near Naples, Italy, in 1887. Neither his parents nor his grandparents could read or write. He was baptized as Francesco and helped on the family's small plot of land as a boy. The family was deeply religious, in the good, medieval way that perdured in rural Southern Europe far longer than it did in Northern lands. Saints, feast days, devotions, processions, fasts, the Mass, angels, saints, the Virgin, and God were the stuff of life. They saturated the atmosphere of Pietrelcina. Little Francesco and his family breathed Catholic air. It entered their bloodstream, circulated in their veins, and oozed out of every corpuscle. When he was about ten years old, Francesco decided to dedicate his life to God as a Franciscan friar. After completing some schooling and being privately tutored, he entered a nearby Franciscan friary at age fifteen. He took the name Pio (Pius) after a saint honored in his hometown. He was ordained a priest in 1910.

Padre Pio lived virtually his entire priestly life at a modest Franciscan friary in the rural town of San Giovanni Rotondo.

Beginning in 1918, he began to experience the stigmata, or marks of the sufferings of Christ. He bled where Christ bled. Holes perforated his hands. He had sharp pains in his side. He also began to display supernatural gifts: bilocation, prophecy, miracles, and healings. His personal routine of prayer and mortification was also stupefying. He did not want his private passion play to go on tour, but it did. He became famous throughout Italy for being holy. Then he became widely known the world over. By the time of his death in 1968, Padre Pio was a bona fide Catholic superstar.

Padre Pio had mystique. That mystique was not rooted in good looks, a chateau on the Côte d'Azur, or in movie stardom, but in how he said Mass. People flocked to witness Padre Pio say long, intense, devotional Masses. In the modern world, sin has mystique. It's cool, retrograde, impulsive, and "edgy." A life of sin and vice is seen as more authentic than a life of goodness and virtue, because the sinner supposedly does not hide his real self behind a social curtain. Padre Pio hid nothing. He was totally authentic, totally sincere, and totally holy. His life was a rebuke of sin. He did not pretend to "share" others' burdens by joining them in sin. He entered into the real drama of life by embodying Christ. A true Christian is authentic when he separates himself and his friends from sin, when he creates the mystique of Christ around him, and when, like Christ, he draws all men to himself.

Saint Pio, your intense love of God was communicated to the faithful in your celebration of Mass, your wise counsel in the confessional, and in your mystical experiences. What was so manifest in you was rare but lies latent in every priest. Help every priest to be an icon of Christ.

September 26: Saints Cosmas and Damian, Martyrs
c. Late third–early fourth century
Optional Memorial; Liturgical Color: Red
Patron Saints of doctors, barbers, and pharmacists

Holy twins are honored for their healing, their poverty, and their deaths

The ancient walls of the Church of the Holy Sepulchre in Jerusalem enclose the sacred ground where the life of Jesus Christ culminated in His death, burial, and resurrection. Both the modest hill of

Calvary and the rock-cut tomb in which His corpse was laid are found under the roof of this venerable church. Calvary and the tomb have long been protected from relic hunters by slabs of marble and stone cladding that conceal the rough, first-century substrata resting just below. There is a custom, still common today, of allowing the faithful to sleep overnight inside the Church of the Holy Sepulcher. From the time the heavy wooden doors close at dusk until they creek open again at sunrise, the pilgrim must remain in the church. This pious custom of resting and watching in the dark, all night long, near a holy site in order to soak up its latent power is called "incubation." The custom originated in an ancient church in Constantinople housing the remains of today's saints, Cosmas and Damian, where the faithful incubated themselves in the hope of a miraculous cure.

Similar to Saint George, legends about Saints Cosmas and Damian far outrun any verifiable historical details about their lives. The devotion to today's saints across epochs and cultures is as broad as an ocean but as shallow as a lake. Upon a slender bed of long-lost documents rests the narrative that Cosmas and Damian were twins and natives of Saudi Arabia who studied medicine in Syria. They became known as the "moneyless ones" for not accepting payment for their healing services. They were likely martyred north of Antioch in the early fourth century.

The earliest historical anchor planting these holy brothers in the ground of history dates to around 400 A.D., when a pagan visitor recorded a visit to a shrine dedicated to Cosmas and Damian in Asia Minor. In the fifth century, a church was built to their memory in Constantinople and, in the sixth century, a pagan temple in the Roman Forum was rededicated as a Basilica in their honor. The bright apse mosaic of Rome's Basilica of Saints Cosmas and Damian still shines and shows Saints Peter and Paul presenting the twins to the glorified Christ.

Most of the wealth of miracles that have long been attributed to Saints Cosmas and Damian involve healing, in keeping with their medical profession. The fame of these miracles, together with their martyrdom, was so widespread in the early Church that they joined that elite class of martyrs, saints, virgins, and popes whose names were inserted into the Roman Canon, or Eucharistic Prayer I, where they are still read at Mass today. Their names also ring out in ancient litanies still sung at solemn Masses. Yet close familiarity with their names may dull our curiosity about their gory end.

No details have been preserved, but it can be supposed that Cosmas and Damian died like so many other martyrs: by crucifixion, beheading, or drowning at sea; by the goring of beasts, or by their flesh being burned off in a roar of flames. The chilling sentence of death read by a Roman official sent a cold shiver up the spine. It was irrevocable. The martyr's fate was often to be publicly shamed, tortured, and physically destroyed in a brutal fashion in keeping with a brutal world. No miracle saved Cosmas and Damian from their violent end. As physicians, they knew well the frailty of the human body. They understood their own bodies to be cracked vessels flooded temporarily with the Holy Spirit of God. And when the time came for that earthen vessel to return to the clay from whence it came, they bravely gave up what was never theirs. They offered a witness so shocking that it was seared into the memories of those who saw it, a witness so other-worldly that a few emulated it, and untold masses of others honored it through prayer and devotion, as we still do today.

Saints Cosmas and Damian, through your heroic witness of martyrdom, we ask your intercession to embolden the weak, to strengthen the hesitant, to give words to the meek, and to unleash the hidden power of the Gospel in all those who could do more.

September 27: Saint Vincent de Paul, Priest
1581–1660
Memorial; Liturgical Color: White
Patron Saint of all charitable societies, hospitals, and leprosy victims

A powerhouse priest organizes multitudes for charity and renews priestly formation

Today's saint was one of the brightest stars in the galaxy of saintly men and women whose light rejuvenated Catholicism in seventeenth-century France. Saint Vincent de Paul established charitable societies that have endured to this day. He also founded male and female religious orders that still thrive in the twenty-first century. He was a trusted counselor to bishops, cardinals, and royalty. His ideas reformed how seminarians and priests were trained so fundamentally that this vision became normative for the world-wide Church. He was the hub of many spokes: a close friend of Saint Francis de Sales, his own co-founder Saint Louise de Marillac, and the almost-saint Pierre de Bérulle. Saint Vincent had a great influence over Jean-Jacques Olier, the founder of the Sulpician Order and a prime mover behind the group of French Catholics who risked everything to found Ville-Marie de Montreal, the explicitly Catholic settlement at the farthest edge of French Canada. Our saint also inspired Blessed Frédéric Ozanam, the lay intellectual who established the Saint Vincent de Paul Societies so commonly found in parishes throughout the world.

Few saints achieved as much as Vincent de Paul. He stood at the core of an evolving group of similarly minded French saints who left an impact like a meteor on the face of the Church. So, although he cannot be understood apart from the charitable Society that bears his name, neither can his achievements be confined to that Society alone. Saint Vincent tried to use his education and personal charm to correct the errors of Jansenism, an overly rigorous spiritual and moral approach to the Christian life that infected wide swaths of the French faithful. When his personal efforts were unproductive, he became more polemical and was instrumental in procuring a papal denunciation of Jansenism.

Our Saint's contributions to the renewal of the life of the clergy were notable. He was a proponent and founder, along with de Bérulle, of the so-called French school of spirituality, which has been so universally adopted in priestly formation that there is, in reality, no other approach. This spirituality combines asceticism, practical and active concern for the poor, a missionary drive to the unconverted, a sophisticated theological education, simple and direct preaching, and a total reliance on the Virgin Mary and the Holy Trinity in seeking to do the will of God. These high ideals, this total approach, also inspired Vincent's near contemporaries Saints John Eudes, Louis de Montfort, and Jean-Baptiste de La Salle to become who they were.

SEPTEMBER

St. Vincent de Paul

To be a man of action and contemplation. To be educated but able to discourse with the simple. To focus on the salvation of souls but also on the material concerns of the needy. To be fully a priest but to have wide circles of lay friends and followers. This was the vision of Saint Vincent de Paul for all priests, and the vision he himself put into action in his own life. He was a force of nature who stormed through life for the glory of Christ alone. Devotion to Saint Vincent followed soon after his death. He was canonized in 1737. His remains are displayed for veneration in a glass coffin above the altar in the ornate chapel of the Vincentian Fathers in central Paris, not far from the chapel of the Miraculous Medal. A partially concealed staircase allows access for the faithful to see the great man up close.

Saint Vincent de Paul, you worked tirelessly for the poor, orphans, and widows. You gathered around yourself numerous helpers. Your primary motivation was not social justice but the pure will of God. Inspire us to be so committed, so dedicated, and so faithful.

September 28: Saint Wenceslaus, Martyr
c. 907–929
Optional Memorial; Liturgical Color: Red
Patron Saint of the Czech Republic and Slovakia

A young duke is killed by a jealous brother and becomes a Czech icon

When the famous die young, their unwrinkled faces, dark hair, and youthful vigor are frozen in time, forever vital, forever attractive, forever fresh. Time is not given its chance to run over their skin like water over rocks. No shaping, cracking, molding or shifting of the surfaces. Before the modern cult of celebrity held up athletes, movie stars, and musicians for supreme adulation, most cultures revered their royalty, soldiers, or holy men and women. Kings and princes, bishops and saints, chiefs and warriors served the common good by governing, praying for, and protecting the people. No class of entertainers distracted a populace from the leadership that mattered. Today's saint, Wenceslaus, Duke of Bohemia, was felled in a fateful encounter with his brother Boleslaus the Cruel. Wenceslaus was already famous when he died young and dramatically. All the ingredients needed to guarantee a lasting legacy were present, and his memory endured. He was recognized by the Church as a martyr, posthumously given the title of King, and quickly became an iconic figure to the Bohemian people such that his Feast Day, September 28, is a national holiday in the modern Czech Republic.

Wenceslaus lived as Christianity was still dawning in Central Europe. German missionaries had been laboring among pagan tribes for a few generations with success, but the visible layer of a Christian culture rested on a rock-hard pagan substrata. Central and Eastern Europe were passing through the normal stages of evangelization, as an age-old culture with all of its customs and traditions was slowly pushed back by a greater force moving across the landscape like a glacier. Catholicism had moved into Bohemia by the 900s, but the religious environment was not yet monolithic. As our martyr's death attests, religious and political divisions still ran through the culture.

The grandfather of Wenceslaus may have been converted by no less than Saints Cyril and Methodius themselves. His grandmother Ludmila was an ardent Catholic and oversaw Wenceslaus' excellent education in which he learned to read and write both Slavonic and Latin. Wenceslaus' mother, Drahomira, clung to the old ways, though she was nominally a Christian. When Drahomira thought Ludmila was encouraging Wenceslaus to assume power as a teen, Drahomira had her mother-in-law strangled to death with her own veil. Once he did take power, Wenceslaus banished his own mother, solidified control of Western Bohemia, and became an honorable ruler. He followed the law, favored education, and promoted the form of Christianity practiced in Germany, not in the East. This was a fateful decision. Poland, the Czech Republic, and Slovakia are Slavic peoples of the Latin Rite, unlike their Byzantine Rite Slavic cousins to the east of the Orthodox curtain. Wenceslaus was pro-Western theologically and liturgically, while retaining his Slavic identity and independence in other essential matters. This double allegiance endures and lends Slavic Catholicism its unique features.

But for all of Wenceslaus' brief successes, in the shadows lurked Boleslaus, creating a power center in Eastern Bohemia. When Wenceslaus' wife gave birth to a son, Boleslaus knew he would not succeed his brother, so he plotted his murder. Boleslaus and his henchman struck down the young Duke Wenceslaus in 929 on the Feast of Saints Cosmas and Damian and on the Vigil of Saint Michael the Archangel. "Brother, may God forgive you" were our martyr's last words.

Saint Wenceslaus, you were the model of a just ruler in your brief reign. You saw it as your sacred duty to promote the true God and His religion. Help all rulers and leaders to see morality, liturgy, prayer, and catechesis as the bedrock of a just society.

September 28: Saint Lawrence Ruiz & Companions, Martyrs
c. 1600–1637
Optional Memorial; Liturgical Color: Red
Patron Saints of the Philippines

A married father remains unbroken under the cruelest torture

Many lesser-known faces in the deep audience of saints bask in the soft glow of sanctity emanating from the more prominent "marquee" saints standing on stage. In the Church's calendar of saints, these more obscure observers of the principle action are often classified as "companions." They can encompass dozens, or even hundreds, of men and women on a given feast day. Today's saint, Lawrence Ruiz, is commemorated along with fifteen just such "companions," in this case mostly missionary priests. Interestingly, Saint Lawrence is not the companion to the priests he died with. The priests, instead, are listed as Lawrence's companions. The married Lawrence is on stage while his companion priest martyrs are in the audience.

SEPTEMBER

Saint Lawrence was born of a Chinese father and a Philipino mother, both of whom were Catholic. Growing up in the Philippines, he served as an altar boy, was educated by Dominican priests, and belonged to a fraternal society dedicated to the Holy Rosary. Because he was an educated and careful writer in a largely illiterate culture, he became a clerk and a calligrapher. He married a woman named Rosario, and they had three children. He and his family lived an ordinary, secure, peaceful life of faith. As 1636 dawned, there was no reason to guess that Lawrence would continue living anything other than a quiet life focused on home and work. But then everything suddenly and drastically changed.

Lawrence was implicated, falsely, in the death of a Spaniard. It was a charge so serious he had to flee the Archipelago. Through his friendships with priests, he was invited to board a ship with three Dominicans, a Japanese priest, and a layman. In June of 1636, the small vessel sailed for Japan, a hornet's nest buzzing with anti-Catholic persecution. The ship intended to land in a peaceful region devoid of persecution, but instead errantly docked in Okinawa at the worst possible moment. Feudal Japanese Shoguns were out for the blood of Catholics, and the missionaries walked right into their tight grip. They spent over a year in prison before, along with still more Catholic prisoners, they were marched to Nagasaki for the inevitable slur against their deepest beliefs.

The Japanese had devised torture techniques carefully calibrated to elicit maximum agony and the renunciation of the faith. On September 27, 1637, the prisoners had huge amounts of water poured down their throats, were covered with boards, and then stepped on by guards, forcing the water to spurt out of their mouths, noses, and ears. Then they were tightly bound, with one hand free in case they wanted to signal renunciation of the faith, and hung upside down over a pit. Heavy stones were tied to their bodies to draw blood more quickly down into their torsos and skulls. As the red liquid painfully pressurized their cranial sacs, the torturers strategically cut the victim's heads to release the collected blood. This prevented the loss of consciousness and prolonged the throbbing pain. Amidst this anguish, no one broke. No one renounced their faith. No one cried out for relief. Mental images of mother and father, of smiling wife and children, of home, the fireplace, and warm embraces, did not prevail. It was God or death. Lawrence's reputed last words were "I am a Catholic and wholeheartedly accept death for God; Had I a thousand lives, all these I would offer to God."

As their chest cavities filled with blood, the victims hearts could pump no more. Lawrence suffocated to death within a day or two. Some of the priests did not succumb as quickly and were beheaded. Lawrence's fifteen companions were Japanese, Spanish, French, and Italian priests; a few consecrated women; and laymen, almost all Dominicans. Their bodies were burned and their ashes scattered in the Pacific Ocean. Lawrence was beatified in 1981 in Manila, the first beatification performed outside the city of Rome. After a Philippina baby with hydrocephalus, or water on the brain, was cured through his intercession, Saint Lawrence was canonized by Pope Saint John Paul II in 1987. He is the protomartyr of the only Catholic nation in Asia, the Philippines.

Saint Lawrence, you were a married father yet forsook return to your earthly home to win a more glorious home in heaven. Help all fathers to be generous in quiet and in tumultuous times, to persevere in small things so they are able to display fortitude in great things.

September 29: Saints Michael, Gabriel, & Raphael, Archangels
Feast; Liturgical Color: White
Patrons of soldiers (Michael); mailmen (Gabriel); travelers and the blind (Raphael)

The air between God and man is thick with mystical beings

It is a principle of Catholic theology that salvation is mediated, that individual man does not go to God alone, and that God does not come to man alone. This means that there are layers of words, symbols, art, priests, nuns, catechists, music, books, churches, shrines, and endless other things and places and people that channel God to us. Even using the name "God" or "Father" or "Jesus Christ" presupposes the mediation of language. So although someone may say they want to "cut out the middleman" of the Church and go directly to God, they can't. At some point in their youth, they absorbed who God was from others, so even the most basic, apparently innate knowledge we have of God is mediated, if only by nature itself. Today's feast is about the created spiritual beings known as angels who fill the space between God and man, communicating His message, protecting man from harm, and battling against the armies of Satan. The Archangels Michael, Gabriel, and Raphael transmit some of God's most important messages.

Michael leads the war cry in a mysterious, metaphysical battle against the Devil and his minions in the Book of Daniel. "There is no one with me who contends against these princes except Michael, your prince" (Dn 10:21), and "At that time Michael, the great prince, the protector of your people, shall arise" (Dn 12:1). Michael means "Who is like God."

Gabriel is an essential figure in the events surrounding the Incarnation. We first meet him in the Jerusalem Temple, announcing the birth of Saint John the Baptist to his father, Zachary: "I am Gabriel. I stand in the presence of God, and I have been sent to speak to you and to bring you this good news" (Lk 1:19). He later conveys the message of all messages to the Virgin Mary, eliciting her "Yes" to God's sublime invitation. Gabriel means "the strength of God."

Raphael appears in the disguise of a man in the Book of Tobit, guiding the young Tobiah along his journey. "…God sent me to heal you and Sarah your daughter-in-law. I am Raphael, one of the seven angels who stand ready and enter before the glory of the Lord" (Tb 12:14–15). Raphael means "God heals."

The Old Testament description of the angels worshipping before the throne of God is one of fierce power:

"…each had six wings: with two they covered their faces, and with two they covered their feet, and with two they flew. And one called to another and said: "Holy, holy, holy is the Lord of hosts; the whole earth is full of his glory." (Is 6:2–3)

These beings are far from the pudgy, pillow-soft, fat-cheeked baby angels so often depicted in art. Today's feast is for the mighty six-winged angels, the deadly serious ministers of God's messages. These Archangels engage in consequential spiritual battle, know that God and His Word are not frivolous, and carry out their missions as emissaries of the Most-High. We invoke them now just as Saint

Patrick did in the fifth century: "I arise today through the strength of the love of cherubim, in the obedience of angels, in the service of archangels, in the hope of resurrection to meet with reward." Amen.

Archangels Michael, Gabriel, and Raphael, we invoke your powerful intercession before the throne of God in heaven. By your spiritual assistance, protect us from harm, heal us of our infirmities, and convey to us God's will for our lives.

September 30: Saint Jerome, Priest and Doctor
c. 345–420
Memorial; Liturgical Color: White
Patron Saint of archeologists, Biblical scholars, and librarians

A prickly scholar translates the Bible into Latin forever and always

Today's saint was living in Antioch in the 370s when he had a vision. Jerome was standing in the presence of the seated Christ, who asked him who he was. "I am a Christian," Jerome responded. "LIAR!" Jesus yelled. "You are a Ciceronian, not a Christian, for where your treasure is, there also is your heart." Jerome indeed loved Cicero and other Latin stylists. The fine prose in their works gave him the greatest pleasure. But Jerome had also been reared in a Christian home, been baptized as an adult in Rome, and had frequently descended into the darkened catacombs to pray at the tombs of the martyrs and saints. His double identity as a scholar of Latin and Greek rhetoric on the one hand, and as a committed Christian on the other hand, dueled within him. Jerome fervently loved God and the Catholic religion with all his soul, but it was a troubled soul. Jerome was full of spit and vinegar. He was a complex man and a complex saint.

Saint Jerome was born in an unknown year in a region northeast of Venice, Italy. His father sent him as a young man to Rome to perfect his education under a famous tutor. Jerome was a superb student and mastered Latin and Greek. At about the age of thirty, he decided to become a monk and traveled to the desert of Syria. For four years he lived a life of austerity, penance, and isolation. He fasted from the classics he loved so much and instead studied Hebrew from a Jewish convert. When he finally came out of the desert, he was ordained a priest in Antioch but never truly exercised any priestly ministry. He studied under the great Saint Gregory Nazianzen in Constantinople and began to publish some translations and biblical commentaries. Around 382 Jerome went to Rome with his bishop to serve as an interpreter and aide. Jerome so impressed Pope Saint Damasus that the Pope then invited the young Jerome to be his secretary.

St. Jerome Writing
Michelangelo Merisi da Caravaggio

At this point, in his forties and while living in Rome, Jerome began the monumental task of translating the entire Bible into Latin from original Greek and Hebrew texts. It would take him years. The existing Old Latin Bible was not cohesive but a jumble of texts stitched together under one cover. Various scholars had generated divergent translations for purely local use. So the Gospel of John in a Jerusalem-based manuscript differed from the same Gospel in a manuscript in Gaul. The one Church, spread throughout the known world, needed one Bible to match its broad scope and theological unity. Jerome was the man for the job. After just a few years in Rome, after the death of his patron Pope Damasus, and due to the enemies his blunt words and fiery temper always seemed to create, Saint Jerome left Rome for the Holy Land. He lived in a cave near

Bethlehem and focused on translating. Some holy and pious women from Rome followed him there and formed a quasi-monastic community around him.

Jerome's translation, known as the Vulgate, became the standard Latin version of the Bible over time, pushing the Old Latin version into oblivion. The Council of Trent formally stated that the Vulgate was the official Bible of the Catholic Church. So Catholicism has a "The Bible," a claim which no other church can make. No "The Bible" ever floated down from heaven on a golden pillow. Except for Jerome's, a "The Bible" doesn't exist. There are thousands of ancient scraps of Scripture from hundreds of ancient texts from scores of libraries and monasteries in dozens of countries, but a publisher and its consultants ultimately choose which texts to include in any published Bible and which to exclude. Catholicism has no such flimsy process. Its sacred word is not dependent on scholarly fashion and whim. It has a baseline.

The Vulgate is like a dropped anchor resting on the ocean floor. It keeps the ship of the Church from drifting. Catholicism is a religion of the Word more than of the Book, but it has a definitive book, nonetheless. The fiery Saint Jerome died peacefully in 420, exhausted from his scholarly labors and life of penance. His remains can be found directly below the high altar of Saint Mary Major Basilica in Rome in a handsome porphyry sarcophagus.

Saint Jerome, you lived a life dedicated to studying the Word of God, to penance, and to prayer. You placed your knowledge and scholarly gifts at the service of the Church which used them wisely. Help all the faithful to serve the Church as much as the Church serves them.

Printed in Great Britain
by Amazon